Edwardian Fashion

Right: Aspects of the Ruritanian scene, when the map of Europe was so different. Here is King Nicholas of Montenegro with his daughter, the Queen of Italy. Montenegro was later absorbed into Yugoslavia. *P. Stevenson*

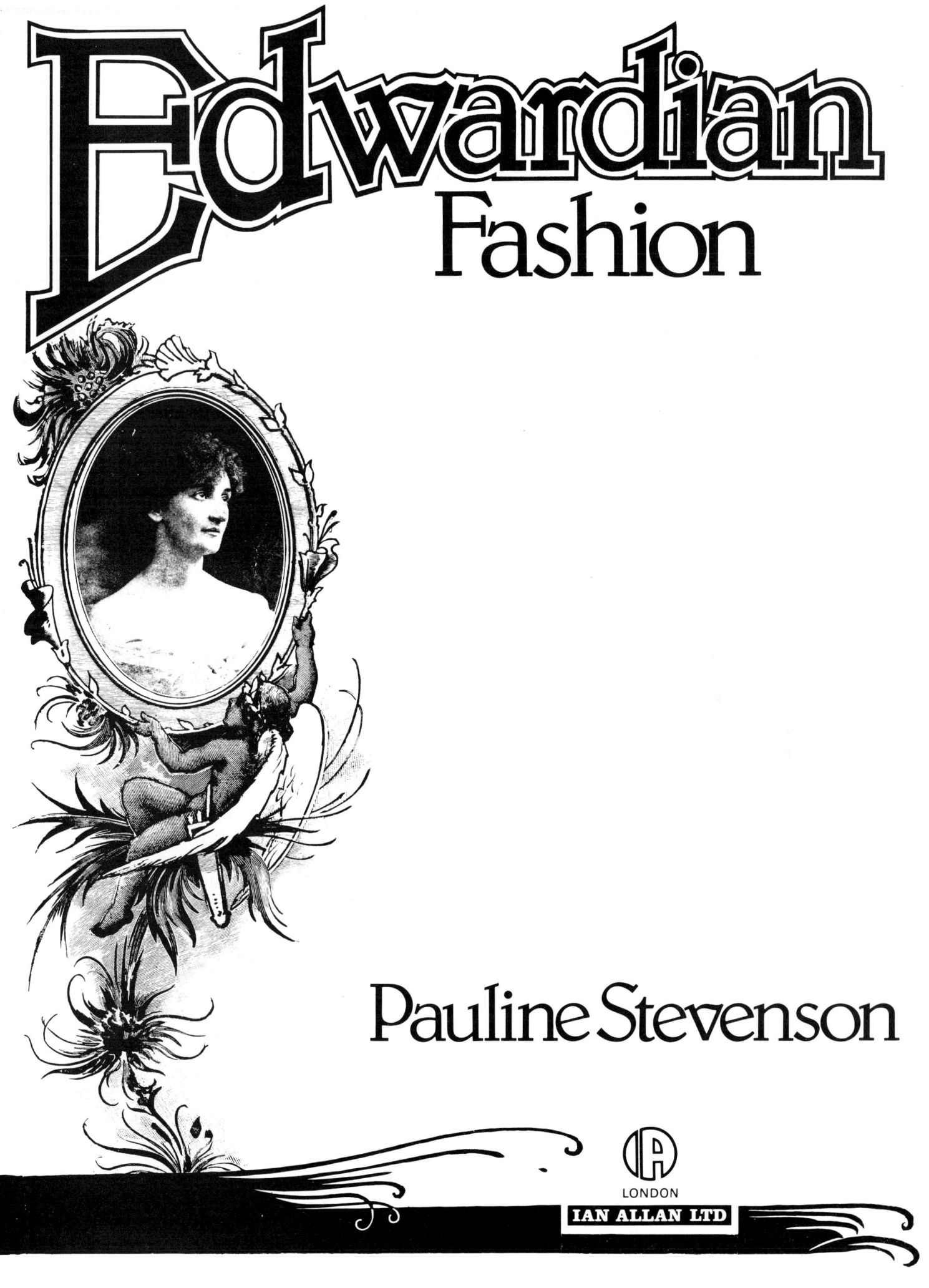

Edwardian Fashion

Pauline Stevenson

IAN ALLAN LTD
LONDON

Right: A bathing costume; The 'Ventnor' a 'becoming' bathing suit in navy and red twill trimmed with white braid at 4/6½d sw and 4/11½d os.
P. Stevenson

First published 1980

ISBN 0 7110 1013 7

All rights reserved. No part of this book may be reproduced or transmitted in any form or by any means, electronic or mechanical, including photo- copying, recording or by any information storage and retrieval system, without permission from the Publisher in writing.

Design by Anthony Wirkus

© Pauline Stevenson 1980

Published by Ian Allan Ltd, Shepperton, Surrey; and printed by Ian Allan Printing Ltd at their works at Coombelands in Runnymede, England

Contents

Introduction 5

Setting the scene: Edwardian Style 6

Women 30

Children 76

Men 108

Front cover: The new status symbol: Edwardian motorists ready for a trip. *Mary Evans Picture Library*

Title page: A group taken in the photographer's studio about 1913: Father in pince-nez, stiff collar and cuffs, boots and trousers with turn-ups, Mother in a cashmere dress and daughter in embroidered muslin with her doll.

Back cover: Mr and Mrs Leonard Bentall and elder son Gerald.
By kind permission of Mr Rowan Bentall

Introduction

For the discussion of the Edwardian style, I have taken the years 1897 to 1914 as the extent of the era. The period starts with Queen Victoria's Diamond Jubilee in 1897. This event, attended by emotional outbursts of affection throughout the country, had a great effect on fashion as the Queen was now regarded as the mother of her people. The huge sleeves, small waist and stiff, outstanding gored skirt suggest the matriarch, and many of the later photographs of Victoria's reign show her in these voluminous styles surrounded by her numerous family and their children and grandchildren. In the last years of her reign, due to her old age and failing health, Edward, then Prince of Wales, was allowed to take on some of her tasks. The personality and character of the future King therefore came well before the public eye, in particular the fashions of his family and followers. Although by then middle-aged he had an obsessive interest in fashion and style and a great awareness of the smallest detail in men and women's clothing. His mother died in 1901, and after the deep mourning period lasting from January to Easter of that year, the matriarchal style underwent certain subtle changes and an altogether more voluptuous woman emerged.

'Fashion is not a trivial thing as is commonly supposed. It deserves the close attention of statesmen and sociologists. Men who refer to it as merely a feminine fancy and a sign of women's superficiality, reveal that they themselves are purblind pendants skating over life in ignorance of its depths. The more deeply is history studied, especially the course of war and revolution, the clearer becomes the importance of fashion and dress.'

These words were written by Sir Basil Liddell-Hart, who besides being a renowned military expert was also one of the greatest experts on costume. Similarly, the great French-writer, Anatole France, said that if, a hundred years after his death, he had to choose one book to discover how life was being lived in the world he had left, he would ask for a fashion magazine which would tell him much more than all the works of historians or savants. In an attempt to enlarge on this theme, I have tried to use as many photographs from family albums as possible, as I feel that, while they are always a source of interest and amusement, they also provide an authentic view of how people looked and behaved — as opposed to the idealised forms of the fashion artist. Readers will realise that this poses difficult problems for the printers as many of the originals are old and faded. I am very grateful to them for their interest and co-operation, and would also like to thank warmly the following people who have helped in so many ways: Lady Liddell-Hart, for permission to quote from her husband's writings; Dora M. Jerman for permission to quote from her diary; Ethel Ellis, Freda Evans, Gladys Stanford, Bunty Waterfield and Joan MacAndrew all of whom have kindly lent me photographs and other material; Ivy Jones for the loan of a christening robe; Ann Potter of Bentalls, Kingston upon Thames, for kind permission to reproduce drawings from Bentalls catalogue of 1912; Christopher Whitmarsh-Everiss, for the loan of engravings and photographs from his collection; Eric and Philippa Archer, for help with photography and drawings.

Above: An afternoon dress and bolero of 1900. *P. Stevenson*

Setting the scene: Edwardian Style

In May 1910 newspapers all over the world vied with each other to express the profound grief and shock felt at the sudden death of Edward VII. He had only reigned 10 years, but in that short time had not only endeared himself to the nation over which he ruled, but had made a deep impression on Europe, Asia, America, Scandinavia and Russia and had influenced the course of history by cementing an alliance with France.

Edward had a sad and frustrating childhood, for his parents felt that he never measured up to what an heir to the throne of England should be. He had little in common with his father, being uninterested in Albert's intellectual pursuits. His mother, Queen Victoria, would not allow him to undertake any work which would involve him in decisions on home affairs or foreign policy until 1893. When he died, however, tributes from all quarters described his tact, diplomacy, knowledge of foreign affairs, statesmanlike qualities, warmth and loyalty to his friends, lovable character as a family man and tireless care for the health and welfare of his people.

His extrovert qualities had made him the most popular of monarchs and his ability to make friends kept him abreast secretly of all that was going on at home and abroad. His intimate friends were the great financiers and bankers of the time like the Rothschilds, Sir Ernest Cassels, who gave him advice in stocks and shares, Baron Hirsch who had made a colossal fortune in railways, and Sir Edward Lipton on whose yacht he frequently took holidays and whom his nephew the Kaiser unkindly called 'his grocer'. These people, the nouveau riche and Jewish financiers, had never been thought suitable to be received at Court in Queen Victoria's time, but Edward both received them and visited them on their luxurious estates in England and abroad. Photographs of fashionable house parties of the time show others of his friends, the unattractive but witty Marquis de Soveral, a Portuguese attaché, and the Duke of Devonshire who under a vague and often seedy appearance hid an infallible judgement and common sense, allied to a great love of sport in the field and in the boudoir.

It was in this racy society, known as the Marlborough House set and at the race meetings, theatres and balls, that Edward, then Prince of Wales, learned what he was prevented from discovering from the despatch boxes, ministerial discussions and interviews which formed his mother's daily routine and which she clung to in her obsessive widowhood because it had formed an integral part of her life with Prince Albert, her most beloved consort.

Because of the marriages of Queen Victoria's numerous progeny, Edward was closely related to nearly all the rulers of Europe. His charming and beautiful wife, Alexandra, was the daughter of Christian IX of Denmark and her sister was the mother of the last Czar of Russia, Nicholas II, who married Edward's niece, Princess Alix of Hesse. The difficult and aggressive Kaiser Wilhelm II of Germany was his nephew; another nephew was the King of Greece. The Queens of Spain and Norway were his nieces.

Top left: King Edward VII walking on the front at Biarritz with the Marquis de Soveral, 1910. *The Mansell Collection*

Bottom left: Edward VII as King — note details of suit, buttons, collar and cuffs. *The Mansell Collection*

Right: Edward VII as Prince of Wales wearing a Homburg hat for which he became famous. *The Mansell Collection*

The map of Europe of those days was of course, completely different from that of today. It consisted, apart from the great empires of Austro-Hungary and Russia, of the fairly recently formed German Empire, the British Empire with its various colonies and India, and numerous smaller kingdoms and principalities, most of whose rulers were related to Edward by marriage. At the time of his death the British Empire was said to stretch from the Falklands in the South Atlantic to the borders of China. Edward, a restless character who loved travelling, had visited large parts of it. At that time France and Russia were in alliance, and Germany and Italy formed an opposing block. England's policy was to maintain the balance of power between them, but it was Edward who foresaw the growing danger of an aggressive Germany and against all opposition and advice went on a state visit to France, then very anti-British, and by his tact and warmth of character converted what could have been a disaster into what was known as the Entente Cordiale.

Although very restless and easily bored, a lover of good living, fashion, and beautiful and witty women, there were other sides to his character with which his subjects identified and for which they loved and revered his memory. His love and affection for his family and for children generally had a big influence on the way

Top: Edward VII as Prince of Wales in a group at Homburg. Note details of costume such as Homburg hats, spats, walking sticks, ties, cravats, also the trim of the beards. *The Mansell Collection*

Above: Edward VII and the Royal Shoot including (from left to right) the Hon Mrs Keppel, the Prince of Pless, Lady Gosford, the King, Lady Desborough, Earl de Grey, Mr Felix Semon and Mr Arthur Sassoon. *The Mansell Collection*

Left: Visit of Edward VII to the Kaiser in 1906; as so often the Kaiser was in military costume. *The Mansell Collection*

Right: A beautiful study of Queen Alexandra in a dress of sequin-covered material. *The Mansell Collection*

the nation thought about children. Remembering his own sad childhood he took care to make his own children happy and to free them from restraints. He and his wife founded hospitals and took a great interest in medical research. It had become very clear when young men were being recruited for the Boer War that the health of the nation left much to be desired. A glance at photographs of this time show thin, badly developed, shabbily dressed youngsters, many of whom were rejected as recruits for health reasons. There were still terrible slums and the too-quickly developing industrial north was indeed the Black Country. One of Edward's jobs as Prince of Wales was to sit on a Royal Commission of Enquiry into the health and conditions of the poor.

King Edward and Queen Alexandra, who during most of their married life were known as the Prince and Princess of Wales, were the acknowledged leaders of fashion. There was no fashionable life at Osborne, Balmoral or Buckingham Palace during the long widowhood of Queen Victoria, but at Marlborough House and at Sandringham or wherever King Edward stayed on the continent, Homburg, Baden-Baden and Biarritz, people in the fashion trade and anyone interested in fashion flocked to note the smallest details of what the royal

Above: Queen Alexandra in 1898 (then Princess of Wales).
The Mansell Collection

couple wore and how they wore it. It has been said that one of the reasons why Edward could go about easily among his subjects was that so many of them resembled him, and certainly all the women tried to copy the beautiful and friendly Queen, even imitating the limp she acquired, as the result of an illness.

The King's wardrobe included suits for every occasion and for every climate, with dress and informal uniforms for every country in Europe with their appropriate orders, sashes, buckles and epaulets, together with hats, helmets, swords, boots and gloves. He was able to give full rein to his passion for detail, etiquette and good form. One was quickly struck off the court list for not appearing in the right costume at the right time or in something unsuitable for the occasion — there was no room for slap-dash apparel. Indeed the fashionable men and women of the time needed a vast amount of clothes and accessories — one could never appear in the same garment more than once at a country house party where the King and Queen were being entertained; it would be noted and remarked on. Every form of activity and entertainment required suitable garments. The women in particular were required to change their whole outfits four or five times a day, and special garments were needed for breakfast, morning calls, shooting, boating, riding, taking luncheon, tea, dinner and going to the theatre. On every occasion, the correct hats (people were rarely seen out of doors without a hat), gloves, shoes, scarves, sticks and parasols were essential. And then there was the jewellery; glittering tight collarettes of pearls, diamonds, beads and cut steel, bracelets, earrings, chains, pendants and

Right: A Royal Family party.
Back row: The Crown Prince of Sweden, Prince Arthur of Connaught, Prince Alexander of Teck with Princess May, Princess Patricia of Connaught, the Duke of Connaught, the Duchess of Connaught, the Prince of Wales, Princess Henry of Battenberg, Queen of Spain with the Infante Jaime, Prince Alexander of Battenberg, Princess Victoria, Prince Leopold of Battenberg, Prince Maurice of Battenberg.
Front row: the Crown Princess of Sweden (Princess Margaret of Connaught) with her children, the Princess of Wales, Princess Alexander of Teck with Prince Rupert, Queen and King of Norway, Prince Olaf, Queen Alexandra, King Edward VII, Prince George, Prince John, Princess Mary of Wales, the King of Spain, his infant heir, Prince Henry, Prince Edward and Prince Albert of Wales.
The Mansell Collection

brooches — enormous hat pins and elaborate fans. All these outfits had their appropriate and very elaborate underclothing. Edward himself had two valets always with him on his travels while two others remained at home hard at work on his wardrobe.

Queen Alexandra had become a fashion innovator as far back as the occasion of her wedding in the 1860s when she refused to follow fashion and wear a crinoline and instead wore a charming wedding gown accurately forecasting the fashion 10 years ahead. Again, at her coronation, she refused all advice on what she and her ladies would wear, saying she knew better than anyone how they should look. How right she was can be seen from the many beautiful studies of her not only in full dress, but in informal poses with her children and relatives. That she was a most loving and affectionate wife, mother and friend is apparent from the many letters written to her and stories told about her.

From the many photographs of the King's state visits abroad one gets an impression of the passion for dressing up in elaborate uniforms that most European monarchs indulged in at this time. At the many military parades, levées and state balls, quantities of medals were given and received and uniforms of extraordinary elaboration and choking discomfort were worn. The Kaiser, who seemed paranoically jealous of his uncle Edward, was particularly susceptible to martial fashion and when he and his six sons paraded in full dress uniform with boots, spurs, epaulets, military cloaks, orders, medals, helmets with fluttering white feathers or in the uniform of the Death's Head Hussars at the head of his troops, it was an overwhelmingly impressive sight. The Death's Head Hussars sported huge busbys with a skull and crossbones on the front surmounted by a tuft of feathers, and severely strapped across the chin. This looked particularly absurd on the German Crown Prince who was rather small and insignificant — one photograph shows him endeavouring to look very martial with this impossible headgear and an enormously long overcoat, booted and struggling against the wind. The effect was enhanced in many cases by bristling waxed moustaches turned up sharply at the ends, or short pointed beards and a triangular clipped moustache. The Kaiser, it was said, imagined himself in the role of his famous ancestor, Frederick the Great of Prussia, whom he loved to impersonate at fancy dress balls. All over Europe, there were very many of these balls in which the guests appeared in elaborate and expensive costumes. One of them, the Devonshire House Ball in England, had a whole illustrated volume devoted to it with photographs and descriptions of the costumes.

It seems more than probable that the King's interest in fashion, good form and style, coupled with his popularity and the desire to please him, may have accounted for the paradoxical nature of the fashions of the time, especially women's fashions. One is struck by the apparent halt to the various liberating influences which had been having a marked effect on women's costume. Women had been gradually breaking free from their bonds, mental and

Left: Queen Alexandra and her daughters. Left the Duchess of Fife and, right Princess Victoria. *The Mansell Collection*

Right: Edward VII with the Kaiser (far right) at Windsor in 1907. *The Mansell Collection*

physical, and in the 1880s there appeared various types of sportswear designed to be functional rather than for reasons of attraction. Women, after having to devote themselves all through the 19th century to the serious business of attracting a husband — marriage being the only career open to them — were beginning to enter many walks of life hitherto closed to them. They went to university, studied medicine, took part in most sports, climbed mountains, drove cars and like Mlle Dutrieu, piloted a flying machine. There were the intrepid women explorers who penetrated unheard of regions of forest and desert, clad in their long skirts, corsets and blouses. The suffrage movement had started and was gaining ever increasing support. These, very often beautiful, but strident women were considered exasperating by many people including the King, who, being all his life a *courreur des dames,* expected women to be women, not to bore him with intellectual conversation, but to be good listeners, minister to his wants, and be objects of beauty and fashion, albeit stiffly

Left: Mlle Dutrieu in 1910 in her flying costume by Bernard.
P. Stevenson

controlled by etiquette. Thus from 1895 on, evolved a type of mature woman (no immature girl was thought anything of) a 'femme du monde' emphasising through her costume all the sexual characteristics of a fertility or mother goddess. Through all history these elements have been the same and consist of abundant hair, a large and protuberant bust and massive hips. In the case of the Edwardian woman the large bust projected and even overhung the tiny waist while the back protruded and the hips were immensely wide in proportion. The effect was obtained by corsets, padded out in all the necessary places, allied to a skirt fitting tightly over the hips with clinging folds around the legs and swishing hemlines from which peeped masses of frilly underclothing made *to be seen.* The boring unsightly underclothing of Victorian days had gone for good. Although women in the King's entourage, and they were copied all down the social scale, endeavoured to please him by forcing themselves into this mould, it appears that many of them were far from happy. The beautiful Lady Warwick, one of his earlier mistresses, defected to Socialism; another friend, the sparkling American Lady Randolph Churchill, edited a monthly review and took up various intellectual and charitable pursuits.

It was no longer considered shocking to become an actress and one of the King's most notorious liaisons was with the exotic Lily Langtry who was received everywhere, even by Queen Victoria. Sarah Bernhardt, a dynamic personality if ever there was one, was a great favourite of the King's. She could truly be called a liberated woman and was always a law unto herself.

So, taking into account Edward's immense popularity both at home and abroad, his feeling for occasion, and his leadership of the fashionable world, it is reasonable to conclude that it may have been his influence which acted as a temporary break on the emancipation of women's dress. Styles after his death veered gradually away from this aspect of sex attraction to an actual anti-sex absorption except for a brief return to these styles after World War II and Christian Dior's 'New Look'.

Miss Camille Clifford, the actress and original Gibson Girl, who left 'The Prince of Pilsen' for 'The Catch of the Season' in 1904. Not a beauty, but the sex symbol of this period.
P. Stevenson

The mother goddess ideal depended for its effect entirely on the corset. The silhouette had changed rather drastically in 1896 from that of the early 1890s which seemed to be a revival of the 1830s showing huge sleeves, a small waist and a stiffly outstanding gored skirt. The new silhouette of the late 1890s which we generally associate with high Edwardian fashion, consisted of a great emphasis on the hipline — protruberant, svelte and padded — a very small waist, sleeves which were tight, straight and slightly puffed on the shoulder line, and a prominent but low and overhanging bust draped with various mysterious frills, laces and ribbons. The skirt had to fit very tightly over the hips so there was no room for pockets, and it flowed down to the knees, then out in wave-like lines showing frothy petticoats.

These effects were impossible without strict attention to the corset and gored skirt. This produced the famous hourglass silhouette which in the 1900s appeared to bend forward and can be seen in the photographs of all the famous beauties of the day, from Queen Alexandra herself to Lady Warwick, Mrs George Keppel, Lily Langtry and Camille Clifford.

The famous illustrator Dana Gibson shows the hourglass silhouette in his drawings of what came to be known as the Gibson girl; as do the artists John Singer Sargent, Boldini and Helleu in their paintings and drawings of famous beauties, American, English and French. These women were magnificent *mature* beings, albeit soft and feminine, who glided rather than walked (constriction making natural walking very difficult) clad in materials and colours which assisted the illusion, and were in contrast to the harsh and ugly colour combinations of the earlier 1890s. In their teagowns and evening dresses they had an unreal, fairylike quality.

The women endeavoured to keep their waists between twenty-one and twenty-five inches. In order to do so, corsets were indispensable and they were made of silk, satin, brocade and coutil, a sort of twill. They came in many colours, black for instance, decorated with small red roses, or in sky blue satin trimmed with black lace and with suspenders (introduced in the 1870s) covered with satin ribbons and with gilt clasps. These suspenders were either attached to the corset or worn on a separate belt over it. Garters were still worn by some women either alone or in addition to suspenders. By 1907/8 the focus of interest was moving from the hips to the bust and the corset as seen in advertisements was getting so long and straight in front it would appear almost impossible to sit down.

If the lady did not have the required shape, and few did, she got into the corset and padded out the deficiencies. Decorated and

frilled bust improvers could be used separately or attached to the corset and these could be padded out to different sizes to get the desired effect.

Under the corset was worn the chemise, a garment which had been in use for centuries, and which now had a very low neck and no sleeves, was lace-trimmed, and generally threaded with ribbon. It usually reached the knees and could be made of lawn, cambric, muslin, Jap silk or any fine material.

There seemed to be a running battle between the chemise, with its popular feminine frills, and the combinations which gave such a svelte appearance to the hips. These combinations were of wool or silk according to the time of year, but cheaper ones could be in flannelette. Next to the corset came the knickers and petticoats the top one often being referred to in advertisements as an underskirt. This was often of coloured silk with much frilly edging designed to be heard and seen. It is amusing to see the pictures of Henley regatta at this time where the men are obviously enjoying wearing various forms of informal clothing, whereas our feminine ancestors are still in tight waists, huge hats, billowing skirts and parasols, languourously arranged on the cushions of boats, or maybe standing up and punting occasionally, an exercise so well adapted to show off the figure to the best advantage! The gored petticoat of 1895 was a *must* for the gored skirt of that date, which was often wired to make it stick out stiffly, and the petticoat had detachable ruchings or fine pleating. This was a practical idea when skirts swept literally over carpets, grass, and pavements alike.

Knickers were of different types. For day wear they were arranged on a band with three buttons at the back and were gathered into a band below the knee which also buttoned. These

Left: A fine example of the black and white drawing of Dana Gibson.
The Mansell Collection

Above: A new way of riding — astride rather than sidesaddle — in 1911.
The Mansell Collection

Right: Ascot, June 1907. Note the parasols, cartwheel hats and veils.
The Mansell Collection

Below right: A garden party in 1908 at Lady Jersey's. *The Mansell Collection*

Above: The opening of the opera season at Covent Garden as drawn by Balliol Salmon in 1909. *The Mansell Collection*

Right: 'Supping the New Year In'. Max Cowper's drawing of the Savoy during the celebrations at the end of 1909. *The Mansell Collection*

could be of cotton, alpaca or flannel and could be coloured — I remember my grandmother in dark blue and white striped cotton knickers made on this pattern. Although India rubber had begun to be used as far back as the 1830s, knicker elastic was not commonly used until about the time of World War I.

There were also the French knickers with very wide legs, frilled and beribboned, which seem to have served no *useful* purpose at all and towards 1906 these became known as divided skirts. Some knickers were made with detachable linings and advertisements show others as fleecy lined. All these seemed to be priced between 3/- to 6/- on average.

Corset covers or camisoles covered the corset and were like a pretty low-necked, sleeveless blouse, embroidered and trimmed with lace and drawn in around the waist with a small basque. As a matter of fact to those interested in fashion revivals, such a garment in black was selling as a blouse for £5 in 1977.

It has been said that the fashionable lady of the period spent a tremendous amount of her time changing her costume for all the different pursuits in which she participated during the course of one day, and this was obligatory in court circles particularly. In order to get some idea of this extensive wardrobe, we will imagine she is about to be married and is choosing a trousseau, in which not only quality but also quantity are the outstanding features together with a hitherto unheard of publicity in which the fashion magazines revel, revealing all sorts of details to their open-mouthed readers, hitherto sacrosanct.

Above: 'The exercise of patience': waiting at the pit door of a London theatre drawn in 1897 by Charles Green RI.
The Mansell Collection

In the year 1907 a reasonably priced Bridal Trousseau would be as follows:

3 longcloth nightdresses trimmed and embroidered with tucks	at 3/9	each
2 longcloth nightdresses trimmed and embroidered with tucks	at 5/9	
2 longcloth nightdresses trimmed and embroidered with tucks	at 7/3	
3 longcloth chemises with trimmed edging	at 2/10	
3 with insertion tucks	at 4/1	each
2 with insertion tucks	at 4/10	each
3 pairs of knickers with embroidery	at 2/5	
3 pairs of knickers trimmed with embroidery	at 3/1	
2 pairs of knickers trimmed with embroidery or 8 combinations	at 3/9	
6 slip bodices with trimmed edging	at 2/2	each
2 flannel petticoats tucked embroidered with silk	at 11/-	each
2 of embroidered silk or cycling knickers	at 7/6	each
2 longcloth skirts plain	at 3/6	each
1 trimmed with embroidery	at 5/9	
1 pair of white corsets	at 6/11	
1 fancy underskirt	at 5/11	
1 dozen towels	at 7/3	
1 chamois band	at 1/-	
1 dozen handkerchiefs	at 7/6	
½ dozen handkerchiefs	at 7/6	each
3 pairs of black hose	at 1/-	each
3 pairs of black hose	at 2/5	each
1 white brilliant dressing jacket	at 5/9	
1 twill dressing gown	at 15/9	

Total £10 13s 9d

A much more expensive Trousseau cost £52 12s and included real lace-trimmed nightdresses, chemises, camisoles and knickers, also breakfast gowns, six pairs of black spun silk hose, cycling knickers, and merino and Alpine vests. At this date came a mention of Southall's and Hartmann's sanitary towels which were 'antiseptic absorbent and disposable at 6d and 2/- per dozen'.

The differing prices of the same articles in these trousseaux refer to the differing qualities.

If one was marrying and going to India, special fabrics could be had on application. Special shops such as the Army and Navy Stores would send out the whole trousseau if desired.

Undergarments ordered in dozens and two dozens were even drawn as well as described and thus we know that the famous American Consuelo Vanderbilt who married the Duke of Marlborough, had 'Consuelo' embroidered on her knickers and other garments. Besides petticoats, knickers and camisoles there were nightdresses, dressing jackets, dressing gowns and teagowns and jackets, stockings, gloves, handkerchiefs, shoes, bags and furs.

Then there were the walking dresses, the carriage clothes, blouses and skirts, clothes for following the guns or for shooting, for golf and tennis, and bicycling and motoring — these latter needing to be dust coats worn with large hats covered by big veils since any vehicle threw up enormous clouds of dust from the unmetalled roads. There had to be a change of clothes for luncheon, and a fascinating teagown for five o'clock tea, when the corset could be temporarily discarded; after which the rigours of the evening were prepared for. After getting as far as the petticoat and bust improvers and camisole, a dressing jacket was donned and the elaborate hairdressing commenced. The hair was brushed and curled with tongs by the lady's maid and was often supplemented by pads and pieces of false hair and what were known as 'transformations', before being decorated by sparkling crescents or stars, tiaras or other jewellery. Then the dinner or theatre dress was put on and with it the jewellery — often a scintillating dog collar tightly enclosing the neck together with earrings, bracelets and corsage ornaments impeccably arranged. Corsage ornaments were frequently composed of jewelled flowers trembling on wired stalks as the wearer moved. Long gloves were worn with evening dresses when the sleeves were short or non-existent or composed of little puffs or frills. Fans of all types, mantles and furs formed part of the trousseau. Chinchilla was a favourite fur often allied to such strange materials as heavy guipure lace. A sable cloak with a large upstanding collar is shown in one French magazine, and about 9-12 inches from the

Above: G. C. Wilmhurst's drawing of the Ladies' Kennel Club in 1904.
Mary Evans Picture Library

Left: Another excellent artist of the day was Frank Craig whose illustration of the Henley Regatta in 1901 is shown here.
The Mansell Collection

Below left: Boating on the River Thames at Richmond, 1915.

Bottom left: American tourists facing the camera at the Pyramids at Gizeh. Drawn in 1909, the illustration shows the increasing fashion of travelling abroad.
The Mansell Collection

Right: Reginald Cleaver's drawing of wild scenes at the Vatican, 1912.
The Mansell Collection

edge is a wide border of very heavy guipure lace about nine inches or more wide. The lady, who may be a model or perhaps a famous actress is wearing a huge rose low down behind one ear. The fashion magazines told ladies that they must not be seen without muffs, that moleskin had made a comeback and that miniver and musquash dyed to resemble seal and even coltskin were fashionable. Feather boas and ruffles were a mania, and nothing could be more seductive allied to the hats and parasols, the long pointed shoes and black suede gloves. White and various soft shades of grey kid or suede shoes would be worn with light summer dresses, and satin and brocade with sparkling buttons and buckles could be used for evening. Soft glacé kid in browns and blacks were suitable in the country. I remember my grandmother holding forth on the relative merits of glacé kid, box-calf and patent leather. The latter two were considered uncomfortable because they 'drew' the feet, she said.

All the hats worn after 1901 were so large and complicated and bore so much varied trimming mixed together that verbal description seems inadequate and many of the various styles are, therefore, illustrated. On the same hat, feathers, whole birds, even seagulls, were allied to huge bows, buckles, fruit and flowers and fur. The hats had to be kept in place by enormously long hatpins which acted like miniature spears transfixing the bulky trimming, hat and hair. These were ornamented in all sorts of ways, enamelled and jewelled, and when not in use had their own decorated container which formed part of the dressing-table set, a long vase-like china or cut-glass affair with a pierced metal top to hold them in place.

It was the job of the lady's maid to see that these huge hats were carefully arranged and pinned into great hat boxes for safe

transit when travelling. They were kept in place by mesh-like structures in the interior of the box, and as the owner probably had to change her hat five or six times over the weekend, the luggage involved for a short stay was tremendous. Luggage was a very important item and the famous American fashion leader, Mrs Rita de Acosta Lydig, carried her pursuit of perfection and beauty into designing special trunks made of Russian leather and lined with cream velvet for her shoes, as Sir Cecil Beaton tells us in his fascinating book *The Glass of Fashion*. Dressing cases and fashionable luggage were carefully made of the best materials with the owner's initials on the lids. Weight was no object as there were always footmen attached to the houses and porters of all descriptions outside ready to earn an honest penny.

No outfits worn for garden parties or indeed any fashionable summer occupation such as Henley or racing, seem to have been complete without a parasol, which at this time was long-handled and obviously used with great effect when pausing to talk or being photographed. The magazines show the ladies twirling them over their shoulders, and elegantly posed with them furled, one delicately gloved hand resting on the handle, the other holding the long trailing skirts in the approved manner. The approved manner was as follows: 'Grasp the edge of the placket hole (of the skirt) with the fingers, do *not* take a whole handful, and lift the skirt up and on to one hip, resting the hand on the hip, and being careful not to turn the elbow out.'

Handbags were made in a variety of fabrics, silks and satins, soft leathers and silver metal rings netted together in the manner of chainmail. The little purses in which the money was kept were often of pale grey leather with a reinforced decorated silver edging.

One advertisement for a small purse handbag in *The Queen*, 1900 deserves to be quoted showing not only where fashion emphasis lay but the amount of space and money available for advertisement then. To quote:

'When women are pocketless, as fashion dictates they should be now, they must perforce fall back on bags, but up to now the difficulty has been that these appendages add greatly to the apparent size of the waist, a consummation which their feminine patrons would not at all appreciate. Messrs S. Fisher of 188 Strand are to be congratulated on the ingenuity and success with which they have met this obstacle by introducing a chatelaine bag that is so curved that it fits into the form of the wearer. It has been patented. It is altogether a clever notion and a perfect success. Within the back of soft, untanned leather is a special receptacle for a purse. It is made in highly glazed crocodile leather with nickel mountings and has a waist belt of the same or with a hook to attach it to the wearer's own waist belt. This is just one of those clever adaptations to the need of the moment that the public know well how to appreciate. This new bag is admirable for daily wear and quite invaluable for travelling.'

One of the questions asked in the correspondence columns of *The Queen* was how to perfume the clothes. The answer was: 'Kent (a nom de plume) would be able to obtain the necessary powder, either violet, Peau d'Espagne or any other scent she may choose from Atkinson, New Bond Street. It is best to scatter a little of the powder between the lining and the skirt, and have tiny little cushions of wadding and powder sewn in under the arms and elsewhere.'

All types of crochet and knitted garments were becoming more and more popular for sporting and outdoor dress and many magazines catered for the home knitter and provided patterns. Examples of long knitted coats can be found occasionally in the pages of French fashion magazines. Knitted Dutch-bonnet style caps were also worn by young women and girls. Blouses figured largely in every trousseau and were of all types, ranging from the strict-looking striped cotton affair worn with a stiff collar and a tie, to every style of diaphanous muslin, frilled, embroidered and

Above left: Winter sports at a German ski resort — R. Gerlach's illustration 1908. *Mary Evans Picture Library*

Above: Cairo in the season — another Reginald Cleaver dated 1905. *The Mansell Collection*

lace-edged. Fashion writers asked their readers 'Whatever did we do without them?'. Over these were worn all kinds of little boleros, some called 'visites', which were also decorated with embroidery and braiding and with appliqué work.

Beading was lavishly applied in embroidery, long fringes going from top to bottom of a dress or hanging several inches deep around a neckline and sleeves, or again on a plaque on the front of the bodice.

Decoration was also applied to stockings which often had open-worked designs in their weave and could be coloured and embroidered; for instance black stockings with a trail of red roses from ankle to knee were most fetching. It is strange to see how many light summer dresses seem to have been accompanied by black stockings of lisle, cotton or wool, although Bentalls' catalogue for 1911 shows some coloured hose.

From advertisements of the time it seems obvious that ladies now used make-up and what is more they did not mind talking about it. In 1900 we read 'Her Majesty the Queen, HRH Princess Mary of Greece, Princess Hohenlohe and HRH Princess Victoria of Schaumberg-Lippe, all use KOKO for the hair and speak very highly of it. The original letters may be seen at the offices of the KOKO Maricopas Co Ltd.'

In 1895 a mixture of walnut juice and nutgalls apparently made good hair dye; eyebrow and eyelash dye possibly of the same ingredients, was recommended. Cream of Stephanotis and Beetham's Glycerine and Cucumber were advised for the complexion, while Atkinson's White Rose Scent, and Vinolia Soap, cream and powder were also advised.

There were advertisements, too, for the cure of freckles and even blushing. One reads 'BLUSHING. A lady whose daughter was cured of this in less than a month will be happy to send particulars to anyone enclosing a stamped addressed envelope to Mrs Williams, No 1 County Chambers B, Marineau Street, Birmingham (mention Myra's).' This refers to *Myra's Journal*, a popular ladies magazine of the period, and the date is 1895.

In the last years of the 19th century one is aware in the fashion plates of these magazines not only of a stiffness in the sharp lines of the silhouette of clothing and headdress, but also of a harshness and stridency of colour and of frequently unpleasant colour combinations. The nouveau riche with no tradition of taste behind them were eagerly showing off their new acquisitions and surrounding themselves with expensive and ugly possessions of all kinds.

As the new century got under way, however, the silhouette, materials and colours became ever more feminine and charming and one is inclined to see here the influence of the lovely and elegant Queen Alexandra who, in spite of many family sorrows, never seemed to lose her kindness and charm, and her unerring sense of occasion and style in dress whether she appears in all the regality of the Coronation or in an informal family snapshot. Her face and figure never lost its beauty, and it was a beauty much more than skin-deep, coming from a warm and loving heart.

In the coloured fashion plates of the time, pale pinks, mauves, soft blues and greens, all shades of grey, buff, and stone are shown in such clinging materials as chiffon, satin-de-laine, muslins and voile, alpaca and panne.

Returning to our bride, she could, if she wished, enter the church in 1901 with her veil thrown back over her wreath and hair, while if she desired publicity no item of the trousseau or detail of the ceremony need go unrecorded. In *The Queen* a whole

Left: Another illustration of travel abroad by Reginald Cleaver — here tourists take afternoon tea and an Italian lesson. *The Mansell Collection*

Below: Reginald Cleaver's delightful holiday sketches from Switzerland, 1902. *The Mansell Collection*

Right: An open-air performance of L'Aventurière by the Comédie Française at Maison Lafitte. Illustration by J. Smart in 1911. *The Mansell Collection*

page would be devoted to photographs; the head and shoulders of her and her prospective husband, their family histories, *drawings* showing the wedding dress, the bridesmaids' dresses, the 'going away dress', the bride's mother's dress, the description of the actual ceremony, the reception and the presents. The list of wedding guests was generally included and the readers were allowed to know where the honeymoon would be spent. All this would have been unthinkable a few years before.

So we see her on her wedding day, her hair elaborately puffed out in front and drawn back behind her ears, surmounted by her elaborate wreath and veil, her neck enclosed tightly in a high collarette of boned chiffon and lace, her splendid bosom a mass of frills, tucks and mysterious overhanging draperies, her tiny waist drawn in and as tightly corsetted as it was possible to bear, and the smoothly outlined protruding posterior descending into a foam of flounces and a sweeping train. Her gloved hands clasp a large and elaborate bouquet.

How beautifully statuesque and dignified she must have looked, but how miserably uncomfortable she must have felt!

A few years later we find the bride as the centre of her family, probably the mother of two or three children. The photograph album shows her posed formally with a child on her lap, her husband holding another child by the hand and perhaps a nurse with a baby in long clothes in the background.

The album shows a number of informal family groups too, enjoying the happy, sunny summer days, taking tea under the shade of the trees and playing croquet on the lawn, or days by the sea, shrimping, paddling, building sandcastles, with a certain amount of rather discreet mixed bathing.

Although children's clothes still appeared stiff and formal in advertisements and illustrated catalogues, it is obvious from the numerous family photos taken by the enthusiastic owners of the new portable Kodaks (which included the royal family) that children were at last being considered as personalities needing far more attention and care than formerly. They were far freer and more informally dressed than their fathers and mothers had been. At the seaside, little girls of six or seven could even run about in jerseys and knickers! This new indulgence can be traced directly to the way the Prince and Princess of Wales brought up their children. Remembering his own constricted and frustrating childhood, the Prince never curbed their high spirits and they were allowed the greatest freedom. High ministers of state were occasionally to be found scrambling about in undignified positions on the floor, attempting to resemble horses, while the unfortunate governesses never knew when lessons would be curtailed or forgotten altogether.

In magazines such as the *Strand* which was considered suitable reading matter for the whole family and indeed catered for any age group, we find the fascinating story of the *Phoenix and the Carpet*, with beautiful illustrations by H. R. Millar. This story, by E. Nesbit, is mainly for the younger members of the family. The children in the story arc all dressed in the clothing suitable for their respective ages, and the dresses, aprons, hats, caps and suits show how these garments looked on living beings. There were in fact, many brilliant illustrators at this period, such people as Arthur Rackham, C. E. and H. M. Brock and Edmund Dulac, to name only a few, whose work, after long neglect, is once again much sought after.

It was fashionable for the fond parents to have prettily illustrated booklets called, for example, 'Our Baby, awake and asleep', in which they recorded the child's weight at birth, when it cut its first tooth, said its first word, took its first step, with places for photographs and remarks enlarging on its capabilities. These books were frequently issued by such firms as Steedman's, who made Soothing Powders, and were charmingly illustrated by coloured drawings.

Babies were dressed in long clothes from birth, and this fashion continued into the 1930s although by that time it was more and more a question of keeping the long robe mainly for the Christening. The child wore a vest next to the skin, then a 'flannel'

Above: **Shortening Day, 1904. Important enough for a special photograph.**

which was like a very long flannel petticoat, only it did not have a seam and was made to spread out flat with small ribbon or braid loops over the arms. The baby could thus be dressed with no discomfort by being laid downwards on its nurse's lap, the arm loops being put over the arms. It was then turned over and the two ends of the flannel were crossed in front, one end being put through a slot under the arm and the two ends tied behind. The long crossed panels of the flannel were folded over in front, turned up over the legs and pinned, thus forming a bag inside which the child could kick its legs. The flannel was possibly a remaining version of the swaddling bands. Underneath it, with the vest, was worn the napkin, and over the flannel was generally worn a white lawn petticoat, embroidered, tucked and trimmed with lace. Then came the white dress decorated in the same manner, but more elaborately and often trimmed with ribbons, blue for a boy and pink for a girl. Over this was placed a short knitted jacket with long sleeves and, covering all, a square light woollen shawl folded into a triangle. The young baby nearly always had a bonnet — necessary even indoors, in days when houses did not have central heating. To be taken to its baptism the baby was dressed in a mantle which often had a short attached cloak, made of a material such as cashmere. Often a small veil was put over the baby's face when in the open air. 'Shortening' took place when the child was about 5-6 months old and was considered to be well established in health and strength. On arrival at this landmark, photographs were generally taken entitled 'Shortening Day' for the family album.

Children of both sexes wore short dresses reaching to just below the knee until about three or four years old, and it is extremely difficult to tell from photographs which sex they belonged to at that age. In many cases the boys' hair is long and curling and tied up with ribbon bows and their frilly dresses are threaded with ribbon. At three or four, the boys were finally put into short trousers with blouses, smocks or little jackets. At this stage the boy's hair was trimmed so that he was recognisably masculine. As he got older the boy progressed through a series of suits, one of the most popular being the sailor suit. (The sailor suit was also worn by girls, but in their case a dark pleated serge skirt was worn instead of trousers.) Outdoors in the summer a large-brimmed straw sailor's hat was worn with ribbon on which was printed the name of a ship; in the winter it was exchanged for a small round serge cap with a ribbon similarly printed.

One of the most common suits for older boys was the Norfolk; very popular in the country and a copy of the sporting man's favourite outfit. Then there was the Cambridge, the Rugby, the Eton, the Parisian, the Clyde, as well as a number of less formal suits for cricket, tennis and cycling. Teenagers appear as formal and stiffly upholstered as their fathers in a variety of overcoats and Ulsters, some with capes. It must not be forgotten that none of these garments for outdoor wear could ever be worn without an appropriate hat or cap. No gentleman or lady appeared in the open air bareheaded and this applied equally to what were called the lower classes and to all those with pretence to respectability. Even pictures of slum dwellers and their children show how carefully heads were covered; sunbonnets, men's caps or tam-o-shanters often being worn by women.

There was much emphasis on masculinity in boys' and men's fashions and in their behaviour and attitudes of mind. No doubt Freud had a theory about it. Possibly it was an attempt to fit our ancestors for the demanding role of empire builders, to make them at all costs manly and impersonal. Even at preparatory school, grammar or public school, the boys were known by their surnames, and if, as often happened, two or three brothers were attending the same school at the same time, the eldest was known as Brown major, the next as Brown minor, the third as Brown tertius and the youngest as Brown minimus. Their father and mother were referred to amongst themselves as 'the Pater' and 'the Mater'. The 'stiff upper lip' was greatly admired and the observance of form regarded as absolutely essential; so that the man who insisted on dressing for dinner in the tropics in some lonely outpost of the Empire, was not laughed at, but held up as an example to be followed. One is struck by the various conversations between men in John Buchan's books, which were referred to as 'rattling good yarns', also revealing are the conversations between boys in Rudyard Kipling's *Stalkey & Co*. 'Service' was the word in this education for manhood: service to King and country, service to those over whom one was called upon to rule as an Imperial power, and service to one's fellow man.

The Edwardian man with his emphasis on masculinity was the perfect foil to the ultra-feminine woman of the period and after a careful perusal of the headgear advertised for a man of fashion one can find no less than 62 different hat and cap styles. Caps were, of course, only possible in the country and the straw hat only became wearable after 1894. For some reason they seemed to denote something not quite respectable; when women started to wear them at the turn of the century they lost their popularity with men. As class distinction was of the utmost importance at this time and their price was within the reach of the majority, it is probable that this accounts for their lack of popularity among the 'upper' classes. The most popular styles appear to have been the Top hat or silk hat (which could be worn with a morning coat, a

frock coat or evening dress), the Homburg introduced by King Edward, The Trilby worn by the actor Beerbohm Tree in a play of that name, and the Bowler which started with a high crown gradually becoming lower. These were known as Derby hats in the USA and could be had in black, brown, fawn or even pale grey in the summer. There were also soft felt hats known as the Wide-Awake and the Alpine.

Hair was worn short with a side parting and any tendency to long hair was looked on askance, marking a man as 'poetic' or 'artistic' and therefore not quite reputable — the scandal of Oscar Wilde's trial still lingered in men's minds. Gloves and canes with different styles of heads were *de rigueur* in town, as were black shoes. No gentleman of fashion appeared in Mayfair wearing brown shoes which were suitable only in the country where they were worn with caps or soft hats, which had such names as the Sans Souci, the Portland and the Clifford.

A fashionable man generally started the London season with about 20 suits which cost him about £5 each, with the exception of the evening suit which would be about £20 each. He was expected to have a fresh coat for every day of the week and changed his clothing three times a day. For instance, he would wear a tweed suit in the morning, in the afternoon a frock coat with a smart waistcoat, and he dressed for dinner in the evening in a black tailed coat, stiff white shirt front and black tie, ending the day perhaps in a smoking jacket or suit. Further down the social scale, young middle-class men could perhaps run to four suits a

Left: A popular style of French picture postcard.

Below: L. Sabattier's painting of motorists reaping the benefits of cheap suburban petrol stations in 1904. *Mary Evans Picture Library*

year. On the whole, colours were drab and this was particularly noticeable on Sundays when everyone went to church; a dark grey or black frock coat would be worn or possibly a morning coat with a waistcoat of the same colour and material, and, of course, a silk hat. The Army and Navy Stores' catalogues which went to every part of the British Empire, on which it was said the sun never set, make fascinating reading, showing every aspect of the life of our ancestors at this time, both by pictures and description and in the case of clothing, the materials, cost and colour are all described and everything is catered for, from birth, through marriage, to death. Bentalls of Kingston also produced some fascinating catalogues, from which examples are shown in this book.

The Edwardians' fashions in neckwear paralleled the other discomforts and tortures which they inflicted on themselves. Men wore stiff high collars which reached their greatest height in about 1899 and were known as stand collars with such names as the Dux or the Shakespeare. This last was a stand-fall with deep points in front completely covering the stand. The stand part varied between $2\frac{7}{8}$ and 3in in height and was adorned with numerous forms of tie and stock for every occasion and state of feeling. The Four-in-hand or the Ascot suggested a certain raciness, while others were named the Edinburgh, the Connaught, the Prince, the President, or the Windsor, presumably made fashionable by various royalty. Some of these collars were of celluloid and could be sponged to save laundering but this was not approved of in the highest circles. With the collars of ferocious stiffness went the cuffs, some detachable and selling for 10/- a dozen. They also had names: the 'Lord Lytton', the 'American' or the 'Westminster', for instance.

The fact that all these accessories had special names points to the enormous amount of time and thought expended on outward appearance and there can be few periods in history in which men and women were prepared to suffer so much for this. Consider the agony, on a hot night in the London season, of a man imprisoned in the starched-stiffened white shirt front of the period with its high upstanding collar and stiffly-tied white piqué bow. Even to tie it oneself was very difficult, as readers of *Peter Pan* will remember.

At the same time, because of the increasing interest in all forms of sport there were mutinous mutterings, and gentlemen were occasionally to be seen in a round hat and a short coat in Bond Street where their friends, and particularly the ladies, affected not to recognise them, or looked hard the other way. There was, however, an ever-increasing desire for comfort and this can be seen in contemporary pictures of Henley where the men have discarded waistcoats and jackets.

The Edwardian girls of the period 1900-1912 look very like their mothers according to the fashion advertisements. The artists drew them with very small waists and stangely prominent busts and hips even at the tender age of eight years old — perhaps it was merely their inability to draw children, a difficult subject at any time. Their hair was long and curly like Mamma's and tied back with ribbons, the curls being produced by rags or curlpapers at night, though patent rubber curlers were being introduced. The dresses reached below the knee and were frilled and embroidered and generally covered with long white aprons which were sleeveless, with a frill at the neck and hem.

On holidays children were obviously allowed more freedom and as the years passed could be seen in bloomers and woollen jerseys digging sandcastles and paddling, the smaller children encased in paddling drawers made of thin rubber or oiled silk, forerunners of plastic.

Ordinarily, however, all girls wore black shoes and woollen stockings with their dresses of whatever colour. A photograph shows a girl of 12 walking to school in a light-coloured, waisted dress with vertically tucked bodice and skirt reaching to mid-calf length, wearing a large floppy hat on her flowing hair and clutching her school bag with white-gloved hands. Young ladies simply did not go without gloves. She is wearing black stockings and shoes. One reason given for their use was that 'they went with everything!' — so economical.

As they got older they looked more and more like mother until the great day came when the family album showed a photograph entitled 'My first long dress'. Of course, the long hair was now put up under a large hat and grown-up corsets were worn which gave the correct hang to the dress. Girls were kept rigorously in the school room until this time and never went to grown-up parties. They were allowed to see suitable plays at the theatre clad in white or very light colours. Violet, Duchess of Rutland, caused a furore in society by clothing her daughter, Lady Diana Manners, in black for a society function, thus showing off her beautiful colouring.

However, families being much larger on the whole, a great deal of enjoyment went on in the family circle with private theatricals, children's dancing parties, charades, picnics, country trips in pony carts and waggonnettes and train excursions to the sea. Roads were not ruined by traffic, beaches were not too crowded nor were towns so densely populated. Here is an extract from a young girl's diary on attaining the great age of 21 in 1912.

'Thursday November 29th 1912. It is Thursday now and since Monday I have been 21. Yet I do not feel as different as I thought I should. I wish I could describe the day, I will try presently. First of all I want to say D. told me her engagement is to be announced today. With all my heart I hope she may be truly happy. Now to proceed with the description of *My Day*. Dear little Auntie came in with all my letters and parcels and we opened them together and some of the letters were so sweet. Father wrote me one from Mother and himself which nearly brought me to tears, but I shall keep it always. Also the ones Sybil, Dick and Walter sent me, they were all such dear letters. [These were letters from a sister, brother-in-law and brother.] At breakfast time a beautiful big

Above left: An Edwardian drawing room showing oriental items from foreign travels.

Above: A country village (Sandford) in Devon showing village children's clothing. Mary Evans Picture Library

posy of Russian violets and maidenhair fern came from the florist. It was from Mother and Auntie. All the morning I was busy cooking etc and preparing for the little supper party in the evening. Aunt Kate, Uncle Charlie, Mrs Carter, Sybil, Dick, Gladys, Dorothy, Clare and Dorothy M. came and after supper we had Charades. (Oh! how we laughed, Father and Dick were so funny.) After that cards, singing and recitations. The supper table looked sweet. It was lighted by eight candles in silver candle sticks and in the centre was silver gauze with the violets sprinkled all over it. Violets were the only flowers and I had crystallized ones on the cake. Dorothy slept the night with me because of catching her train in the morning which she only did by the skin of her teeth! We had a good talk together. I had some lovely presents, altogether 25! Father and Mother gave me a gold signet ring, and my set of seal coney furs, they are beautiful and I can't help seeing they suit me. The muff is a Granny one. *Sybil and Dick* gave me a sweet little antique, gold brooch. *Amyas* [her brother] a beautiful engraved gold blotter. [ie engraved with gold from Liberty.]
Walter and Nancie [her brother and sister-in-law] a beautiful volume of Browning.
Auntie, a picture, and a charming blouse length [Japanese].
Clare. Japanese antimony trinket box.
Dorothy, Two volumes of Music, one of Chopin.
Dorothy's Mother and Father An ebony manicure set.
Mrs C. and Ella Charming pendant and hatpin.
Uncle William and the girls Set of four books of Kipling.'

So we get a glimpse of a happy middle class family and their obvious affection for each other two years before the Great War had changed their lives. The young woman who wrote this diary then became one of the first female bank clerks to be seen in her native city of Exeter.

Beyond the description of furs, hatpin and pendant there is unfortunately no description of what she wore. She tells me, however, that she thinks the dress may have been a present from her friend, Ella, at that time training to be a teacher at the Royal Holloway College whose mother was accustomed to making her three new evening dresses for the beginning of each new college year, presumably nine dresses in all. This suggests that the students at this date were not always the rather dreary 'bluestockings' one pictures, but had quite a social life. At any rate she has described one or two of her own attractive dresses made by someone in Exeter who described herself as a Court dressmaker, and these were made between 1912 and 1914.

One was her first ball dress of soft cream silk with a draped bodice and big cream satin sash forming a hobble skirt which was then the fashion. She danced in it, but one wonders how!

About 1913 she had made, at her father's special request, a charming soft pink satin dress with a low neck and draped bodice, the skirt caught at the sides with pearl embroidery motifs and tiny puffed sleeves with the same embroidery and a pink tassel. Now aged 87, she tells me that she had a scorching time at dances in this!

Then there was the dress made for a winter wedding reception in 1913. It was a long coat frock of cedar green French face cloth with long tight sleeves cut to a point over the hands. This had a plain bodice but on the left side the skirt was slashed open showing an under panel of plain cloth to just below the waist. This slashing was edged with cedar green braid which was also used to trim the side of the bodice and the wrists. It was, she says, beautifully cut and wore for years. She wore it with a small fur hat and matching fur stole. Her father, it seems, took a great deal of interest in her clothes and she used to accompany him on various occasions, her elder sister having married.

Just about this time, ie 1912, Diaghilev's Russian Ballet opened in London after first stunning, and then fascinating Paris audiences, and this had a very far reaching influence on the colour and line of young women's clothes. There was a marked tendency to harem skirts, a very much higher bust line and much less emphasis on the corset. The mature woman was gradually fading out and a younger sylph-like being was taking her place.

Strangely enough, huge hats were still being worn but with not

so much mixed trimming. They were softer in line and made usually of a great deal of draped and gathered material, particularly velvet. The various trends showed an aping of masculine styles in morning dress and in sportswear, with various tailor-made coats, blouses with high stiff collars and ties, and knitted jackets, while in the afternoon and evening a tendency towards French Directoire styles intermingled with Russian and Oriental themes is evident.

The great French designer, Paul Poiret, was now at the height of his powers and most of his designs at this time bore a very Oriental stamp, relying on turbans with upstanding feathers, materials in such contrasting colours as pink and orange, purples, greens and blue and all shades of yellow, layers of various transparent drapery, long strings of beads and tassels. Designs could be in the Chinese, Japanese or Turkish style while a number of classically-draped dresses were trimmed with Greek embroideries.

While Poiret himself said that none of his designs owed anything to the influence of Diaghilev's genius, it is rather hard to believe this. Of course, he became famous at a time foreign travel and cosmopolitan ideas were becoming within the reach of everyone, travels which King Edward VII had done much to make popular, as he was the first monarch to go on these extensive world tours.

These oriental themes did not appear overnight and another glance at the family album will make it plain that the older men and women still clung to the older styles while other, younger members of the family were eager for more freedom and variety which the new styles were able to give. Strident as were the Suffragettes, they nevertheless appeared frequently on public platforms in charmingly feminine styles, and by no means all adopted mannish clothes and stiff collars and ties, with dauntingly severe hats. Perhaps, therefore, we can sum up the period between 1909-1914 as a period of transition, comparable to those periods in architecture when the older styles can be seen imperceptibly changing into the new.

Above: A very early design by Poiret when he worked for the designer Doucet, about 1896-7. *P. Stevenson*

Right: A suffragette poster c1905. *The London Museum*

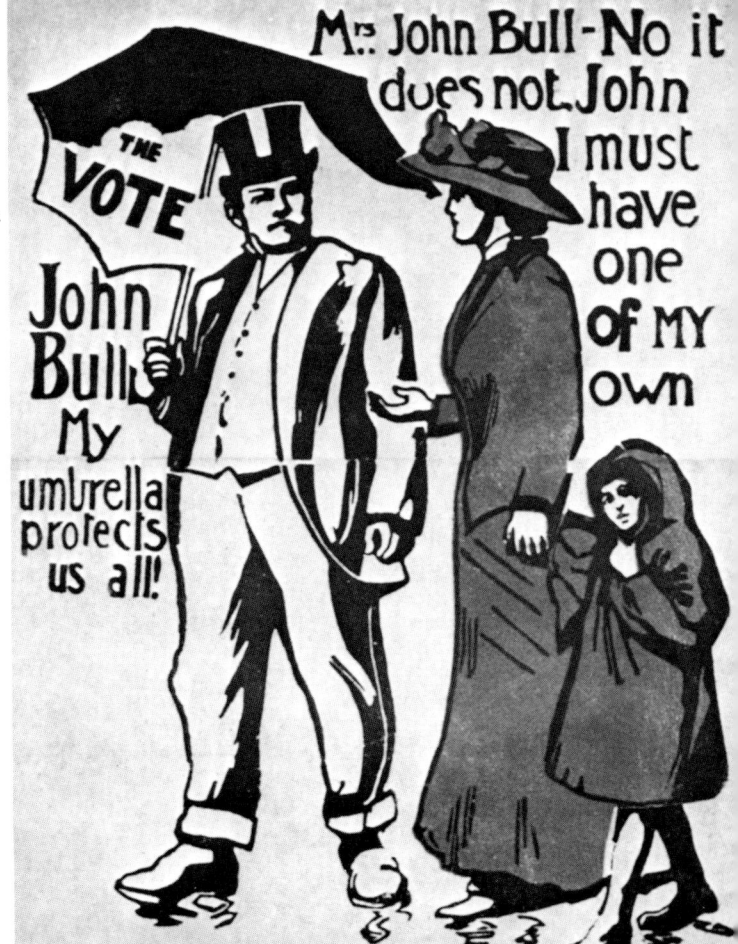

Edwardian fashion accessories such as jewellery, hair ornaments, textiles and embroideries, show the influence of an important art movement which swept Europe at this time. It was known variously as Art Nouveau in England, Jugendstil in Germany, Le Style Moderne in France, Stile Liberty in Italy, Modernista in Spain and Secession in Austria. It is obviously impossible within the scope of this book to deal with the complete artistic scope of this movement except briefly in the context of fashion.

It is thought to have had its roots in England in that extraordinary character, William Morris, who would have probably disliked its eventual manifestations very much, but its later most famous British exponent was the Scotsman, Charles Rennie Mackintosh, who designed the Glasgow School of Art and the famous Willow Tea Rooms for a Miss Cranston in the same town, carried out between 1897 and 1912.

The movement gained very much more impetus and indeed many more adherents in Europe than it did in England. In France many houses and more than one metro station, not to speak of a host of smaller objects of all types and for all purposes, were designed for the great Paris Exhibition of 1900.

Here could be seen the most luxurious personal adornments — beautifully wrought hair combs, in such materials as gold, enamels, jade, obsidian and opals, and pendants, bracelets, collarets and rings. Some of the jewellery designed for Sarah Bernhardt by René Lalique making use of the elegant shapes of dragonflies and incorporating her beautiful face in translucent enamels can only be described as fantastic. Much use was made of baroque pearls and semi-precious stones such as moonstones, peridots, rosequartz, as well as mother-of-pearl.

Henri Van de Velde in Belgium while designing interiors, furniture and silverware also tried to design some dresses based on these themes. They were not a success and the style as far as clothing went seems to have lent itself best to embroidery and textile design. The sweeping and curvilinear shapes of the hats and dresses may have owed something to its influence especially as shown on the covers of some fashion magazines, but as shown in a photograph on a rather heavy Germanic figure of the period it looked far from attractive.

The style spread to America where some of the most unusual glassware, known as Favrile glass, was invented by Louis Comfort Tiffany, the son of the jeweller of *Breakfast at Tiffany's* fame. He catered for the newly rich, fashionable world of New York, but his son had travelled and acquired taste and training in art.

By this time there were many families in New York whose immediate ancestors had made fortunes in all forms of industry and had leisure and money to follow the trends in London and Paris. As far as clothes were concerned they followed mainly what they saw in London adapting the styles to the differing climatic conditions. For instance, air conditioning was not yet invented and so in the summer much lighter materials were needed as the summers were hotter than in England. Similarly the winters were much colder and then far heavier materials were absolutely necessary. Many more fur-lined coats were worn by both men and women, and on the whole, as far as men were concerned, a looser style of cutting was apparent, as was a certain flamboyance in the colours and accessories that would have been frowned on in London Society, then carefully modelling itself on King Edward.

Paris fashions were copied by the wealthy New York ladies but elegant English women thought they lacked dress sense. One such, Lady Duff Gordon, who arrived in New York about 1910, had her own fashion showrooms under the name of Lucile and her designs can be seen in many contemporary fashion magazines showing haute couture. She is reputed to have been the first English designer to have seen the importance of showing her clothes on live mannequins whom she recruited herself and

Below: A fine drawing of Phil May showing 'Street Arabs' dancing to a barrel organ. *Mary Evans Picture Library*

trained in deportment. On the staircase of her house in Hanover Square these beautiful young women descended and ascended like fashionable angels, showing off her ethereal designs to an enthralled audience below. She brought these lovely girls over to New York with over one hundred of her latest creations which were greeted with extravagant praise. When describing her designs, she often used language reminiscent of Eleanor Glyn, the famous authoress of *Three Weeks*, who was, in fact, her sister.

Some of her models went on to appear in the famous Zeigfeld Follies of the time and later she designed costumes for these productions. Her influence was immense and longlasting and the famous designer Molyneux owed much of his success to her influence.

We have already made some mention of Art Nouveau and its influence in America. It is probable that it was widely disseminated by the work of an extremely talented Austrian named Joseph Urban whose work is little known in England. Randolph Carter in his book entitled *The World of Flo Zeigfeld* shows some fascinating examples of his designs for the sets for Zeigfeld's shows. The impact of his ideas and the shapes and colours of these works of art, must have had much the same impact that Diaghilev's Russian ballets had had in Europe.

In the realm of literature, very popular at the time were books about the 'Ruritanian' scene portrayed for example by Eleanor Glyn, Marie Corelli, Anthony Hope and others, and so wittily and amusing derided by Sir Cecil Beaton in his book *My Royal Past or the Memoirs of the Countess von Bülop*. The fabricated land of Ruritania was a small principality or kingdom somewhere in Europe, where the most exciting and romantic events took place, involving political intrigues, dastardly plots and romantic love affairs between persons with elaborate unbelievable titles and equally unbelievable costume. The novel *Three Weeks* deals with such a plot involving a beautiful and mysterious lady fleeing from a wicked husband, and a handsome young Englishman, her lover for three weeks. There seemed to be a vast amount of rolling about on tigerskin rugs and beds of roses which absorbed the contemporary reader in delicious thrills and excitement, the books, of course, being carefully hidden from the children.

The male actors in these dramas were frequently clad in the various complicated uniforms of the day which could actually be seen all over Europe and particularly in Germany. The passion for dressing up in extreme discomfort appears to have been boundless and there seems to have been no large or small state which did not have its quota of elaborate military styles which never appeared again, except at military parades, after the Great War of 1914, when khaki had finally taken over.

Another side of life which also disappeared with the Great War was the world of the demi-mondaine.

Anyone wishing to know what a demi-mondaine was and how she was trained for her exalted position has only to read *Gigi* by Colette. The nuances of behaviour expected of a highly sophisticated and expensively maintained mistress are explained here in detail.

The ladies themselves appear frequently modelling clothes in the foremost French magazines of the time, though sometimes their names are omitted. They had beautiful houses and apartments, carriages and horses, the best jewellery and clothes and every form of luxury, *only* they were never received into Society. If seen to be dining with the man who kept them, or together anywhere else in public, the couple were invisible to his friends and relatives. Everyone knew of their liaison but it was never referred to. These women were, however, a great source of income and advertisement to the great couturiers who were able to show them in their latest and most startling or most beautiful creations, at race meetings, balls, theatres and fashionable restaurants. Occasionally their careers ended in marriage, but not often. Everything depended on their making enough money and amassing enough jewellery at the zenith of their career, so that they could retire gracefully, as in the case of Gigi's Aunt Alicia.

Sir Cecil Beaton's *The Glass of Fashion* has a most entertaining chapter about them and anyone who has the chance to study the French magazine *Les Modes* can see them immortalised in photographs. As Beaton pointed out, they existed mainly in Paris, but there were nevertheless a few in London.

Many people think that the death of King Edward VII marked the end of an epoch, but it is perhaps more realistic to see it as a short Indian summer between the Victorian years and the cataclysmic horror of World War I. Sir Basil Liddell-Hart said that fashion accurately described the feelings and aspirations of a period and, indeed, this is true of the fashions of the Edwardian era. By the end of Edward's reign, the opulent discomfort and sexual allurement of 1901-5 was disappearing and the much more informal and straighter fashions were taking their place. Although the dresses were becoming easier to wear, the hats were at their widest in 1910. Even if the Great War had never taken place, it seems that attitudes of mind and the different way of life would have brought about a change and fashion accurately mirrored these changes. It also expressed in a way no words could, the depth of feeling for Edward VII throughout the nation, when at the race meeting at Ascot a short time after his death, men and

Below: A typically sentimental postcard of 1915.

MEET ME TO-NIGHT IN DREAMLAND (1).
Dreaming of you, that's all I do,
  Night and day for you I'm pining,
And in your eyes, blue as the skies,
  I can see the lovelight softly shining.
Because you love me there it seems,
Pray meet me in the land of dreams.

women one and all appeared from head to foot clothed in black.

The effect must have been astounding; a great sea of black waving feathers on enormous black hats, black boas and parasols, black top hats and trousers and umbrellas, rustling black silk and black gloved hands. The only light note being the white papers from which to study form and lay bets.

So ended one of the most popular reigns in history. One in which the monarch was closely identified with his people; not only with their ideals, but also with their failings for which they loved him all the more. His character emerges as very human, warm and endowed with tact — a word scarcely understood today — and with the ability to dissolve many an ugly international situation. For instance there are those who maintain that had he been alive in 1914 World War I could have been avoided.

In the history of fashion we glimpse in this brief period, scintillating, exciting and luxurious styles which have never been repeated since.

Menu at a Ball Supper (at Round Tables) including Light Refreshments served at the Buffet throughout the evening at 7/- per head for 50 persons, including attendance and use of all necessary tables and chairs, plate, glass and china, cutlery and table linen. 1/- per head extra if all supping at the same time.

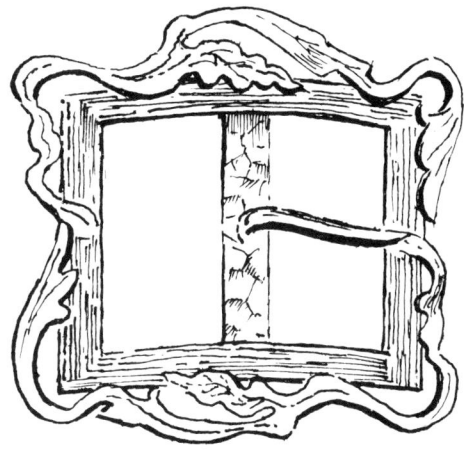

Lobster Salad   Aspic of Prawns
Roast Boned Turkey
Braised York Ham   Roast Chicken
Boiled Chicken à la Béchamel
Galantine of Veal   Galantine of Tongue
Braised Ox Tongue   Aspic of Eggs
Raised Game Pie   Braised Beef

— ★ —

Sherry Jelly
Strawberry Cream   Pineapple Cream
Macedoine of Fruit Jelly
Fancy pastry
Meringues with cream
Dessert

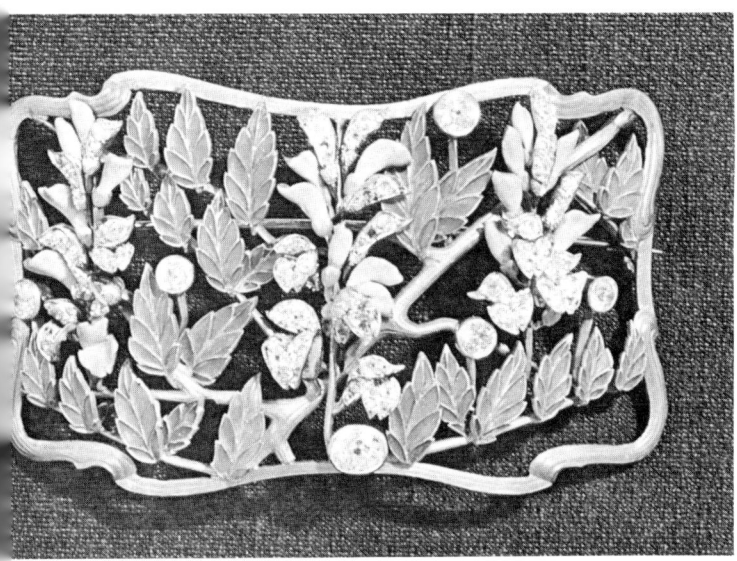

Three examples of art Nouveau jewellery: Above, a belt buckle in silver and enamel, 1903; *P. Stevenson,* **below, a plaque from a collar — gold set with diamonds decorated with plique-a-jour enamel, c1900; bottom, a brooch — gold enriched with translucent enamels.** *Victoria & Albert Museums*

Ices served at Buffet, Strawberry cream and Lemon Water. Also at the Buffet, Tea, Coffee, Bread and Butter, Cakes, Biscuits, Lemonade, Soda Water, Claret Cup and Ices.

Consommé served at Buffet on departure, altered according to the season.

Menu du Diner
for fourteen persons at 20/- per head

Hors d'Oeuvres
Fausse Tortue Claire
Creme d'Asperges

— ★ —

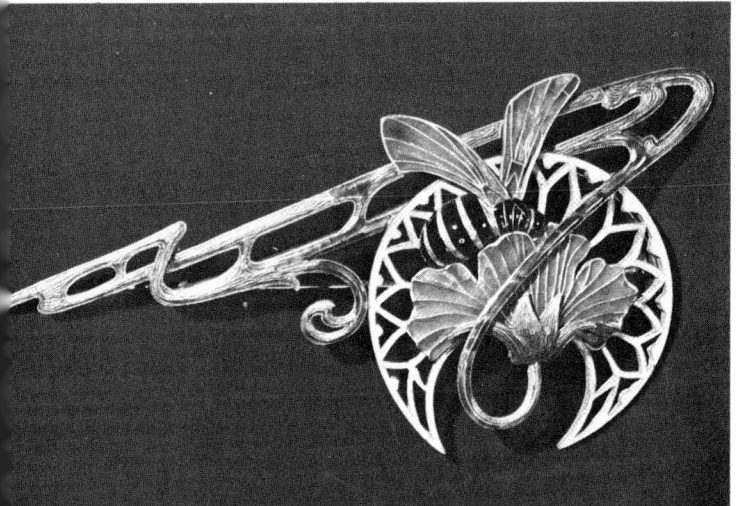

Filets de Sole à la Cardinal
Blanchailles
Ris de Veau à la Toulouse
Cailles en Turban

— ★ —

Selle d'Agneau
Jambon de York à la Macedoine
Canetons aux Petits Pois
Petits Poudings à l'Alexandra
Canapes à la Sinclair
Glacés
Desserts
(according to the season)

Women

Above: Mabel Turney wearing a pretty blouse and wide suede belt.

Left: A drawing from a family album entitled 'My first long skirt'. This would also be the time when the hair was put up.
P. Stevenson

Above: Visiting relations in the country at Sandford, Devon.

Above: The first ball dress was important enough to warrant a special visit to the photographers and several different aspects of it were recorded.

Far left: Miss Sybil Jerman in her first ball dress, wearing long white silk gloves. Note the hair ornament and fan. The dress was pale pink with lace insertions.

Left: Emily Jerman c1914.

Right: Entitled 'My first ball dress and wrap worn at the Bachelor's Ball held in the Public Rooms, Exeter'. c1903.

Below: A French actress taking a bow on stage. Note the jewellery.   *Philippa J. Archer*

Far right: A page from Bentalls' catalogue for 1912 showing white embroidered ready-to-wear robes.
This and other catalogue pages reproduced by kind permission of Bentalls Limited

COSTUME DEPARTMENT.

WHITE EMBROIDERED Ready-to-Wear ROBES.

Our new Blouse & BLOUSE ROBE SALON is replete with the latest Models for the Season at Special Prices.

The Designs shown are faithfully reproduced from the Garments themselves; they are not in any way exaggerated.

R911.—4/11½
The Marvel, Embroidery Frock, Fine Tucked Front and three-quarter sleeves Magyar style.

Recent Extensions in this Section gives us Increased Scope for Business.

R915.—6/11½
White Muslin Blouse, Magyar Sleeves, low neck, Tucked Allover, trimmed with Fine Valenciennes and Embroidery.

R914.—6/11½
Smart Robe of White Muslin and Broderie Anglaise. Special price.

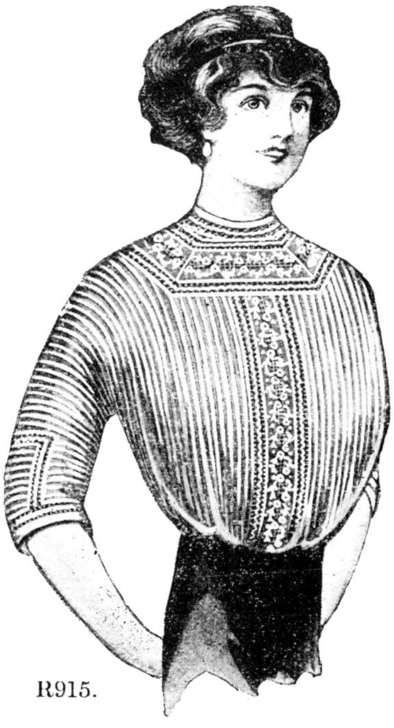

R912.

R915.

R916.—12/11
Stylish Robe of Allover Embroidery, beautiful design. Marvellous Value.

R913.—12/11
Charming Frock of White Muslin, Handsome Embroidery Top Tunic effect.

LADIES' TAILORING.

Perfection in Fit Guaranteed.

R912.—11/9
Dainty Robe of White Muslin and Broderie Anglaise, Peter Pan Collar. Special Value

BOOTS THAT LOOK AND WEAR WELL—See Pages 185-198.

Above left: Charades and private theatricals were very popular. Note the small purse on the chair back, the hair styles and jewellery of the three sisters.

Above centre: A beautiful Oriental dress made at home for a fancy dress ball c1907. This was made by a visiting dressmaker. Worn by Miss Dorothy Lake of Exeter.

Above right: Another fancy dress worn by the same young lady.

Left: More private theatricals c1908. This scene was entitled 'the Gossips' and a special programme was produced for it shown here (bottom left).

 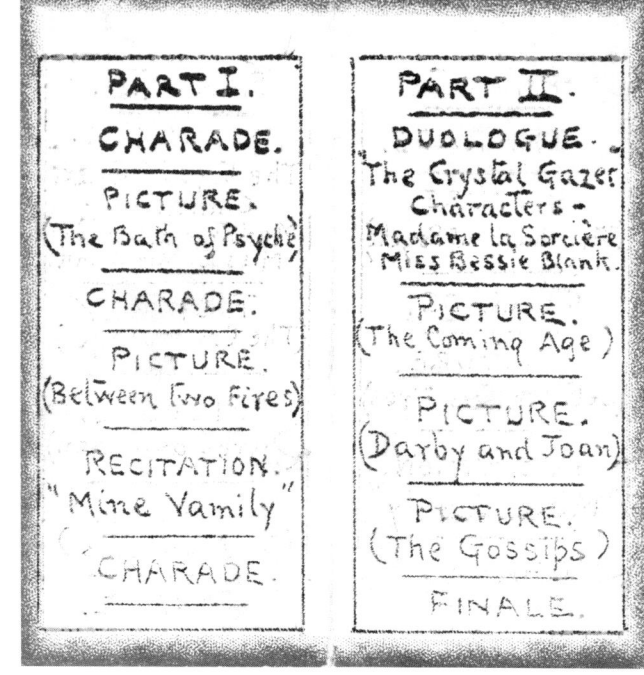

FRANK BENTALL — 60 Separate Departments. — KINGSTON ON THAMES.

GOWN DEPARTMENT.

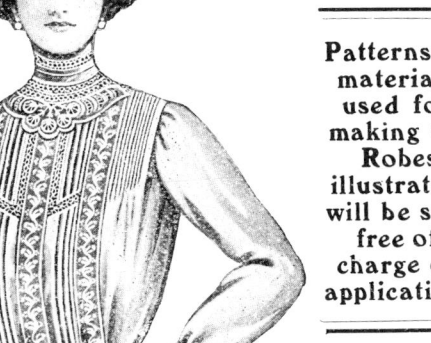

Dainty Wash-Frocks of the latest designs and colours, all British made goods.

Patterns of materials used for making the Robes illustrated, will be sent free of charge on application.

B361
White Muslin Blouse. Of marvellous value, long Sleeves, Valenciennes yoke, embroidered Motif and Front.

B361.—1/11¾

B8112
Blousute, made in a new printed Hair Cord. Bodice is made on broad line effect edged with White Embroidery to fall over shoulder, and piped plain material to match Gown. V-shaped neck, opening finished off with Collar of tucked Nainsook and embroidered Cuff to match. Sleeve is a Magyar set in Sleeve. Skirt has a wide band of Embroidery going round.

B4172.—5/11½
Casement Sute. Bodice with Embroidered Reveres and lace vest. Set in Sleeve finished with Lace Cuff, Skirt with Tabs of Embroidery front and back.

150 White Embroidered Ready to Wear Robes, Dainty Designs, Special Price, 8/11½

B3212
Blousute, made in striped Reppiqué. A very simple style of garment which has the so much favoured pointed effect on Bodice and Skirt. Blouse as well as Skirt is carried out with side panels of plain pique interrupted by slashings of material, & trimmed buttons. The Yoke consists of plain white pique

B3212.—15/11

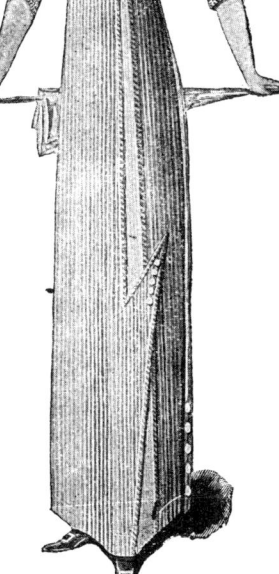

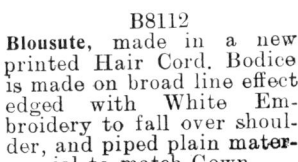

B8112.—18/11

Very Smart Princess Robes of Fine Coating Serge. Trimmed Black Military braid and Piped with Satin in Shades of Emerald, Saxe, Self and Black, Bentall's Price 18/11

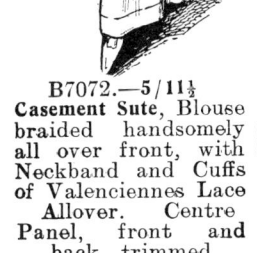

B7072.—5/11½
Casement Sute, Blouse braided handsomely all over front, with Neckband and Cuffs of Valenciennes Lace Allover. Centre Panel, front and back, trimmed buttons

B7212.—12/11

B7212.
Zephyrsute. Bodice tucked in sets, with inlets of chain effect Zephyr Embroidery. Vandyked shaped Yoke of white embroidery, finished with Valenciennes Lace Collar. Waistband with Embroidery Loops. Plain Skirt, finished with side tabs of Embroidery and bands of same running round.

DON'T MISS THE FURNISHING PAGES 241-306.

FRANK BENTALL — PERFECT SATISFACTION OR MONEY RETURNED. — KINGSTON ON THAMES.

Gown Department.

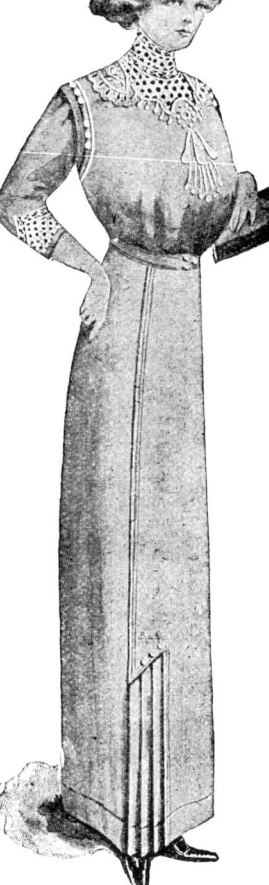

Beautiful Collection of French Lace Robes and Tunics for Day and Evening Wear.

Wonderful Value in Coloured Wash Frocks. Splendid Assortment to select from.

B7172.—9/11
Blousute in Plain Zephyr. This garment has a square bodice finely tucked, with centre pleat trimmed with buttons. The neck has a square collar effect, is embroidered in spot and wave lines. The Embroidery is also carried out on the sleeve, round cuff, and on the waistband. The Skirt has an embroidered centre panel, which is shaped with a scolloped one-sided effect.

B118.—7/11½
Magyar Sute, in Plain and Striped Zephyr. Peter Pan Collar of plain material trimmed Beading and bordered with Stripe, finished with tie to match. Turn-back Cuffs. Skirt very plain, with Beading and Stripe, cut on the cross running round back.

B706.—12/11
Zephyr Frock, Blouse front Embroidered in a novel bead effect. Yoke is made of a new net effect, and trimmed round shoulder with Medallions of White Embroidery. Lace Collar and Cuff. The Sleeve is set into Piped Bodice. The Skirt has a front-shaped panel, and is finished off with side pleats.

Large Assortment of Nurses' Uniform Dresses at Special Prices!

B2012.
Blousute in Plain Zephyr. V-shaped Vest of Valenciennes Lace, bordered with a fancy-shaped Sailor Collar, and finished with a Sailor Knot. Skirt has Panels of Stripe let in, V-shaped fashion, finished with buttons.

Housemaid's Ready-to-wear Dresses in Cambric and Oxford Shirtings, from **3/11½** complete.

B0172.
Morning Frock, Blouse consisting of a square effect. The Embroidery is formed of Motifs picked out alternately in striped design. It comes down over the Sleeve as well as at the back. Skirt tunic-like at the front and back, and finished with Flounce Sidepleats.

B2012.—9/11   **B0172.—10/11**

FIVE CHARMING MODELS, AND AT SUCH PRICES, TOO!

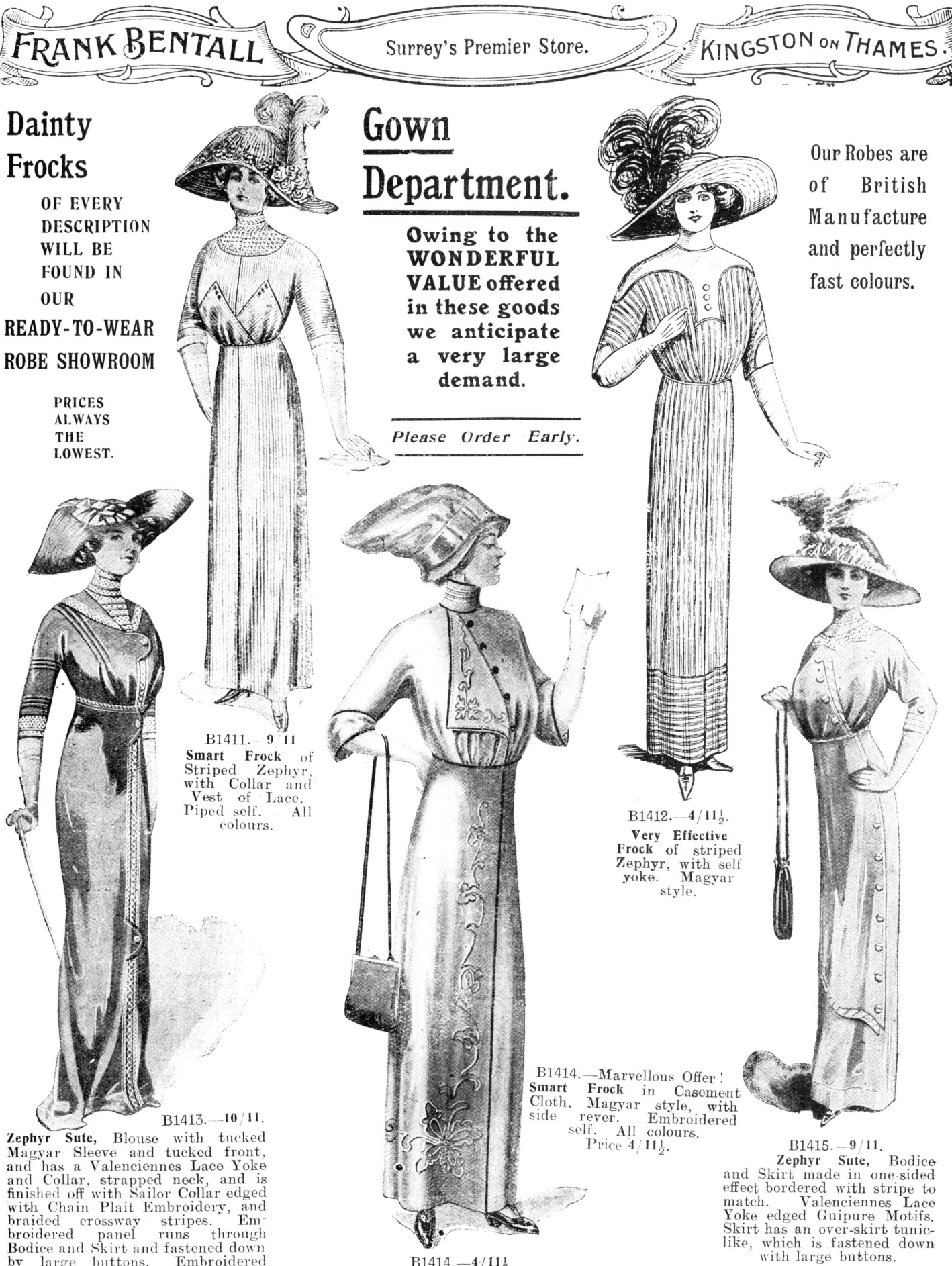

GOWN DEPARTMENT.

DAINTY FROCKS FOR DAY AND EVENING WEAR ALWAYS ON VIEW AT BENTALL'S.

Our Dressmaking Department is thoroughly organised to turn out Gowns of every description at most reasonable Prices. Perfect Fit Guaranteed.

Mourning Orders executed on the shortest notice. Patterns and Estimates Free.

B1511.—Smart Washing Gown made in fashionable White Pique or Linen over Tunic, Black and White stripe skirt, White Embroidery vest and sleeves and Leather belt.

B1511.—29/6

B1512. — An up-to-date Cotton Voile Gown, tunic of Fancy Voile to tone overskirt, trimmed silk Fringe, dainty Lace Vest.

B1512.—29/6

Special line of Navy Serge Dresses, Piped various colours, Magyar style. 10/11

B1513.—Smart Dress made in Navy Serge, trimmed black braid. Wonderful Value.

B1513.—21/9

B1514.—29/6
B1514.—Lace Frock carried out in heavy Guipure Allover with shaped inset of tucked fine Net Lace on Bodice and Skirt.

Charming Frocks of Black and White Stripe Taffetta, Piped Emerald, Cerise, Royal and Black. Wonderful Value, 29/6

B1515. Stylish Gown in self striped wool Taffetta, trimmed Black and White, silk and embroidered motifs.

B1515.—21/9

Below: A beaded afternoon gown about 1906.
P. Stevenson

Above: The young lady of the diary (see p24) in 1913.

Right: An attractively embroidered dress in 1911.

Below: Portrait of an Edwardian beauty, Mrs Clarke.

FRANK BENTALL — Surrey's Premier Store — KINGSTON ON THAMES

COSTUME SKIRTS.

Tailor-made Skirts in Cream Serge, Linen, Drill and Pique at Special Prices.

Large assortment of Skirts in Voile, Silk and Velvet for smart wear.

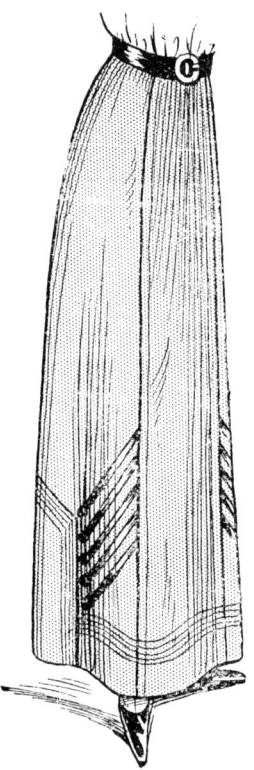

CS2011.—6/11½
Tailor Cut Skirt in Black and Navy Serge, lengths 38, 40, 42ins.

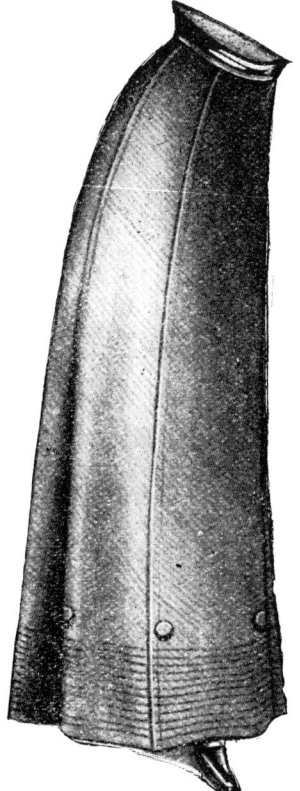

CS2012.—5/11½
Useful Skirt made in Cheviot serge. Black and navy all sizes.

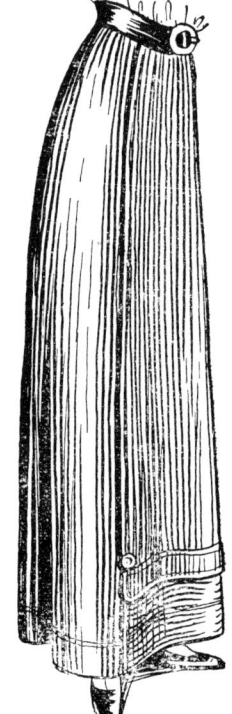

CS2013.—10/11
Smart Skirt of New Spring Tweeds, stripe effect. Special Value.

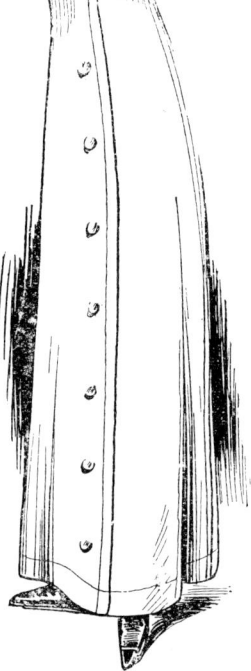

CS2014.—12/11
Smart Skirt made in Cheviot serge. High waisted, trimmed buttons, Cream and Navy.

CS2015.—12/11
Tailor Made Skirt made in navy and black coating serge, panel trimmed braid.

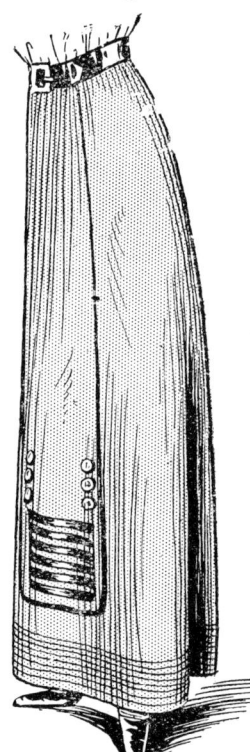

CS2018.—14/11
Very Serviceable Skirt of black and navy serge, trimmed buttons, special value.

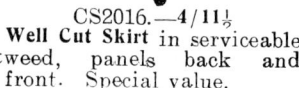

CS2016.—4/11½
Well Cut Skirt in serviceable tweed, panels back and front. Special value.

CS2017.—7/11½
Tailor Made Skirt of coating serge, trimmed braid and buttons, perfect fit.

Euphoric descriptions of tea-gowns from *Country Life* of 28 September 1907 by fashion correspondent Lamia.

'For any woman making her round of country house visits, the tea-gown is quite as important an item as the tailor-made costume. Indeed one might almost say more so, for certainly gorgeous variety at the witching hour of tea is more appreciated by the returning sportsman as he stretches his tired limbs in the depths of a luxurious armchair than the neat cloth suits which achieved a general grunt of approval when the women joined the guns at lunch in the coverts. It gives a man a sort of luxurious feel of being an Oriental Pasha, as he lies in his chair, smoking the ever-present cigarette, to see himself surrounded by graceful houris clad in gauze and gorgeous draperies, shimmering with rainbow colours; for as George Meredith has told us "Men have got round Seraglio Point but they have not yet doubled Cape Turk". For the delight of their eyes, therefore, do we devise such charming creations as our artist has sketched on our second page, and which would suggest dreams of houris when viewed through the blue cigarette smoke after a long day with the partridges.

'The long plain fourreau of maize Liberty soft satin is cut somewhat on Empire lines and has a little bodice of maize chiffon crossed at the breast and held by two bands of satin. The full sleeves of the chiffon are simply tied at the elbow with maize velvet ribbon. Over the satin robe is a long sleeveless coat of coarse filet net, edged all round with a narrow band of sable or mink fur and embroidered all over with a large pattern of conventional roses in every shade of brown and copper in heavy silks interspersed with brown and copper irridescent tube sequins at intervals. The rich colouring of autumn is expressed in this beautiful but simple gown, while the note of symbolism which is one of the most subtle fascinations of the tea-gown finds utterance in the brown faded roses of the silk embroideries. Of all opportunities which the art of dress gives to a woman to enhance her attractions and make herself seductive and beautiful, there is none that can more emphasise all types, for it knows no laws.

'There is the queenly type which can express itself in gorgeous brocades of gold and silver and heavy Venetian lace; there is the lissom type that can glide into the firelight "clothed in white samite that more expressed than hid her"; there is the splendid Bacchante type whose tea-gowns will generally recall in some subtle way the wine-coloured draperies, panther skins and vine leaves of her forbears running through the olive woods of Ancient Greece and Sicily; there is the fair Undine type whose faint green and white draperies shimmer as with the foam of her fountain; one and all can find in the tea-gown the expression of their intimate type if they are lucky enough to possess one or clever enough to invent one, the latter often the better one of the two, being cultivated with the greater art. The tea gown is the freelance of the world of dress. Any eccentricity will be accepted therein, so long as the effect is successful and becoming; it may unite the colours of the rainbow or glimmer in the twilight in Quaker grey; and in the tea-gown the imaginative woman comes into her own. I had intended to describe some beautiful tea-gowns I have lately seen for the autumn campaign of country visits, but space fails me this week (!) *and it is but to reculer pour mieux sauter* and I shall hope to describe some beautiful tea-gowns coming over from Paris next week.

'Other things which must not be forgotten for the autumn campaign are the Sachets de Toilette and Sève Dermale of Dr Dys. One may have the loveliest and most symbolic of tea-gowns in the world, but if the neck and arms they disclose are dull and leathery in colouring and texture, the effect will be entirely lost. The little sachet should be soaked in a basin of hot water and its contents squeezed out making a milky perfumed lotion to which should be added a tablespoonful of Sève Dermale, and in which the face neck and arms should be bathed for ten minutes night and morning. This process will keep the skin as smooth as velvet and as white as a camellia, without any use of pernicious "make-up".'

Left: The popular Teagown which is described in very high-flown language in the text, and comes from *Country Life* magazine.
P. Stevenson

From Anthony Trollope's *The Vicar of Bullhampton* regarding the heroine's friendship with her cousin.

'In America a girl may form an intimacy with any young man she fancies and though she may not be free from little jests and good-humoured joking, there is no injury to her from such intimacy. It is her acknowledged right to enjoy herself after that fashion and to have what she calls "A good time" with young men. A dozen such intimacies do not stand in her way when there comes her way some real adorer who means to marry her and is able to do so. She rides with these friends, walks with them, and corresponds with them. She goes out to balls with them and picnics with them and afterwards lets herself in with a latchkey, while her Papa and Mama are abed and asleep, with perfect security. If there is much to be said against the practice, there is something to be said for it. Girls on the other hand on the continent of Europe do not dream of making friendships with any man. A cousin with them is as much out of the question as the most perfect stranger. In strict families, a girl is hardly allowed to go out with her brothers; and I have heard of mothers who thought it indiscreet that a father should be seen alone with his daughter at a theatre.

'All *friendships* between the sexes under such a social code must be looked forward to as post-nuptial joys.

'Here in England there is something betwixt the two. The intercourse between young men and girls is free enough to enable the latter to feel how pleasant it is to be able to forget for a while conventional restraints and to acknowledge how joyous a thing it is to indulge in social intercourse in which the simple delight of equal mind meeting equal mind in equal talk is just enhanced by the unconscious remembrance that boys and girls when they meet together may learn to love. There is nothing more sweet in youth than this, nothing more natural, nothing more fitting, nothing indeed more essentially necessary for God's purposes with his creatures.

'Nevertheless, here with us, there is the restriction, and it is seldom that a girl can allow herself the full flow of friendship with a man who is not old enough to be her father, unless he is her lover as well as her friend.'

Interesting, but possibly somewhat naive remarks, one feels from a Victorian writer and had he happened to live longer he would have found these restrictions still in force up to 1914.

Below: A family group at Biarritz c1913.

Right: Young woman bank clerks in Exeter c1914–1915. The diarist mentioned in the introduction is second left in the front row.

Left: Two 'Visites' which were types of bolero generally of chiffon and lace worn over the bodice of the dress which would make the dress look more exciting and dainty. The sleeved 'visite' is in two shades of lavender and violet, trimmed with passementerie and braid. About 1906, for afternoon visits. *P. Stevenson*

Right: The wedding of Mr and Mrs F. R. Rowley of Exeter in June 1909. The bride's dress is of soft white satin trimmed with true lover's knots and worn with a wreath of orange blossom made of waxed flowers. The various details of the bridegroom's costume should be noted.

Below: An Edwardian wedding group about 1909. The bride's dress is at present in the R.A.M. Museum, Exeter.

Below right: The bride and bridegroom from the same group. Note the train corsage ornament and attractive bouquet also the details of the bridegroom's costume.

Left: A winter outfit from Les Modes 1901, consisting of a black velvet skirt, a short coat of leather and chinchilla fur and a muff of lace velvet and chinchilla, surmounted by a hat of felt and velvet decked with acorns and oak leaves. Probably worn in a carriage for visiting.
P. Stevenson

Right: In fancy dress; this time an original dress of 1840 of pale grey cashmere with a swansdown muff and shoulder cape.

Below: Crossing by the ferry in 1899.

Right: Informal country clothes for a walk to Brentor Church, Dartmoor. c1901.

FRANK BENTALL — 60 Separate Departments. — KINGSTON ON THAMES.

MANTLE DEPARTMENT. Eminent Rain Coats.

Mars.—21/9

Lennox.—21/9

Madras.—18/11
Smart Rain Coat of Cravenette Coating, in Grey, Fawn and Greeny Fawn.

Mars.—Fine Sports Coat of Ementine Cloth. Raglan Shape. Also half lined check, **25/9**

Lennox.—Cravenette Rain Coat. New Shape. In Grey, Green, and Fawn Coating, **21/9**

Aden.—Smart Raglan Coat of Cravenette Coating and Ementine Twill. Special Value, **21/9**

Paris.—Smart Rain Coat of Ementine Coating. Latest Shape. Unlined, **18/11**
Half lined check, **21/9**

Aden.—21/9

Paris.—18/11
Half Lined Check, 21/9

Far left: Three ladies in a garden c1902.

Left: A family group in the garden c1902.

Below: Two demi-mondaines clad in what were known as demi-toilettes enjoying 'le thé' and a chat outside a café on the boulevard about 1906. *Philippa J. Archer*

Far left: A sable evening cloak with a broad inset of guipure lace. The hair is dressed with long combs set with pearls and with a large rose set low on the nape of the neck; French 1901.
P. Stevenson

Above left: A family picnic on Dartmoor about 1903 showing various styles of hats and caps.

Left: A dog show in 1906.

Below: The Woodmans entertain old friends to tea in the garden at Joanpaynes, Pinhoe, Devon, 1904.

FRANK BENTALL — LUNCHEON AND TEA ROOM FIRST FLOOR — KINGSTON ON THAMES.

FURS.

F3311.—**Long Coney Wrap**, as sketch, lined silk. 18/11. Large pillow Muff to match, 10/11

F3312.—**Black Hare Stole**, 72 ins. long by 9 ins. wide, lined satinette, 10/11. Large Pillow Muff to match, 8/11½

F3313.—**Special Coney Wrap**, soft bright skins, good effect. 28/11. Large Pillow Muff to match, 21/11

F3314.—**Smart Natural Squirrel Wrap and Muff**, both lined squirrel locke and trimmed tails. A very effective and durable set. Complete, 5 guineas

F3315.—**Dark Kolinsky Stole**, as sketch, trimmed real tails. Solid skins. 57/6

F3316.—**Coney and Caracul Wrap and Muff**, lined silk. A very elegant set. 4 guineas

F3317.—**Dark Sable Fitch Princess Stole**, lined silk, with fancy open end muff to match. The set complete, 4 guineas

F3318.—**Natural Squirrel Scarf**, 20 skins, lined Merve Silk, trimmed tails, 28/11. Large Pillow Muff to match, lined silk, 25/11

WE DON'T FOLLOW THE LEADERS, WE LEAD THE FOLLOWERS.

Above: This lady is covered with livestock with paws, tails and a head. The best part of some huge bird rests on her head enwrapped in two enormous velvet bows. The furs are described as being of topped sable with a 4-6 skinned muff to match. The muff cost £32 18s 6d and the furs £40 15s. *P. Stevenson*

Top right: Severe styles for walking in 1910. The lady second from left is French.

Above right: A family group near Bridestowe, Devon in 1912. Here the young ladies have discarded their hats.

Right: Clothing impedimenta to climbing in the Swiss Alps in 1909.

Left: A bizarre mixture of the masculine and feminine in the yachting outfits for 1900: (a) In pale blue serge with braiding and embroidered anchors; (b) In white serge with navy braiding and navy tie.
P. Stevenson

Below: Hilarious mixed bathing at Broadstairs in 1914.

51

Three bathing dresses from Bentalls' catalogue for 1912:

Left: A swimming costume in navy stockinette trimmed with white braid and anchors.

Centre: The 'Margate' in navy alpaca trimmed with white braid at 3/11¾d sw and 4/6d os.

Right: The 'Calais' described as an exceedingly smart costume, a combination shape with skirt of navy serge and white braid at 6/11½d, 7/6½d and 7/11½d.
P. Stevenson

A cycling dress and hat of 1903 and two motoring hats.
P. Stevenson

Cycling in 1902, showing short skirts of tweed, one is bordered with leather. *P. Stevenson*

Left: A lady's riding hat and stock of 1909.
P. Stevenson

Right: This riding habit made by an Exeter tailor was originally knee-length but the riding master insisted that the skirt should be lengthened as shown in case his pupil had to walk through the town c1914.

Below: A tennis group at Cranborne, Dorset in 1908. *P. Stevenson*

Above: A winter hat in 1900. Fur animal tails emerge from sparkling horseshoe clips, while a long brooch of enamel and brilliants fastens them in place. The hat is of felt edged with satin.
P. Stevenson

Right: Black alpaca and a white feather-trimmed hat c1903.

Below right: An engagement photograph in 1906. A serious affair!

Below: A country drive in 1906.

Contemporary pictures showed men at the seaside constantly peering through telescopes or binoculars, but these were not always trained on distant ships. *Mansell Collection*

Left: Ladies walking costumes, 1897. Note the sleeveline and hats.
Mansell Collection

Right: How to appear at the Seaside from *La Mode Illustré*, 1899.
Mary Evans Picture Library

Left: 'Je pars' or an English version might read 'Back to Mother'.
Mary Evans Picture Library

Below left: At the barbers, c1900. Note the décor and early hairdryers.
Mary Evans Picture Library

Right: Sleeveless wrap of sea-green chiffon showing the top-heavy silhouette of this date from the *Ladies' Field*, 1911.
Mary Evans Picture Library

Above: A hat designed by Maria Guy and drawn by J. Gosé.
Gazette du Bon Ton 1912-13

Left: An illustration by A. E. Marty showing an afternnon dress by Dœuillet.
Gazette du Bon Ton 1913

Right: Tailored walking costume drawn by J. Gosé.
Gazette du Bon Ton 1913

Above: Early French aviators draw a crowd at Bétheny in France, 1909.
Mary Evans Picture Library

Right: A summer hat of 1901 made of white satin with silk gauze-stiffened bows of pale blue trimmed with pink roses.
Philippa J. Archer

Above: Fair hair, blue eyes and a pearl necklace c1912 — Miss Gladys Wooster.

Right: A postcard 'pin-up' girl in 1912.

Below: For spring 1901. A hat with stiffened black lace brim trimmed with a large black velvet bow on which are set two long curved buckles set with brilliants. For good measure is added a bunch of primroses and some curled ostrich plumes!
Philippa J. Archer

Above: A French evening headdress of Art Nouveau design of enamel, diamonds and topaz. The design is based on fern fronds 1901. *P. Stevenson*

Left: A summer hat for 1900 of coarse straw trimmed with large red poppies and a pink silk scarf. *Philippa J. Archer*

Below: A sentimental Christmas postcard of 1913 with plenty of mistletoe.

A hat of green folded straw for the summer of 1902 trimmed with white flowers and mauve velvet ribbon.
Philippa J. Archer

HAIR REQUISITES.

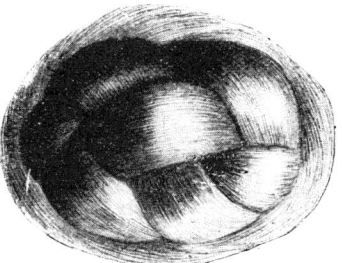

H20.—To sketch, Ordinary Colours 21/-.
Light colours and Grey extra.

H30.—Single Puff, 10¾d each. Best French human hair only used in first quality.

Best French Human Hair only used in all articles of our Manufacture.

H40.—Swath Dressing, 26 in.
3-stem switch required for same.

These Prices apply to Medium and Dark Colours only.

Quotation for other Shades post free on application.

Estimates given for making up, pattern of Hair should always accompany orders.

H50.—Marie Stuart Frame. Long natural wavy hair. 10 in. 5/11. 12 in. 6/11.

Real Human Fringe Nets, 2¾d, 4¾d, 6¾d.
3 Sizes. All Colours.

H60.—La Ruche Cluster of Curls for back dressing. 12/11 each.

Real Human Fringe Nets. Special line.
3 for 1/0¾. 6 for 1/11½.

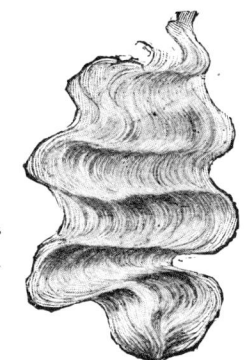

H10.—Pin Waves
size 1 1/11½,
size 2 2/11½.

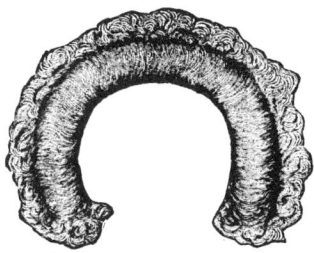

H90.—Real Hair Frame.
10 in. 2/11½. 12 in. 3/11½.
Short Hair.
These prices apply to medium and dark colours only.

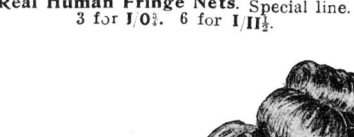

H16.—3 Stem Plait.
22 in. 13/11
24 ,, 15/11
26 ,, 18/11
Cheaper Quality.
22 in. 8/11
24 ,, 10/11

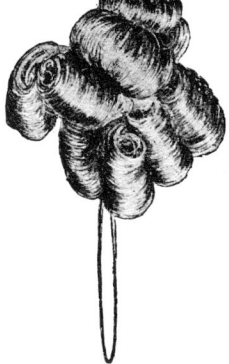

H70.—Top Curls, 2/11½.
Cheap Quality, 1/11½.

H14.—Switch.
Switch Stem.
Best French
Hair Switches
16 in 5/11
18 ,, 6/11
20 ,, 7/11
Cheaper Quality.
16 in. 3/11
18 ,, 4/11
20 ,, 5/11

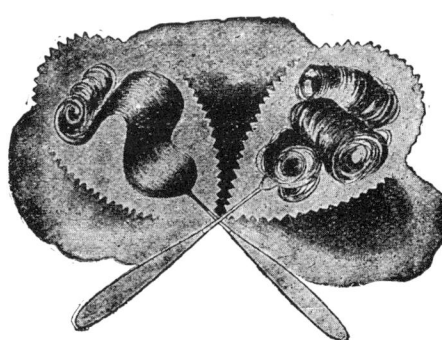

H100.—Pin Curls.
Size 1, 9¾d. Size 2, 1/0¾.

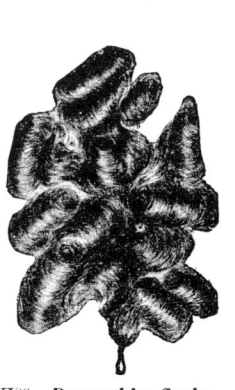

H80.—Devonshire Curls,
4/11½. Large Clusters,
8/11. Cheap Quality 2/11½.

FRANK BENTALL — ORDERS BY POST RECEIVE EXPERT ATTENTION — **KINGSTON ON THAMES**

HAIRDRESSING DEPARTMENT.

Best Quality Hair Frames.
Real Human Hair Covering, Fine Wire Bound Edges.

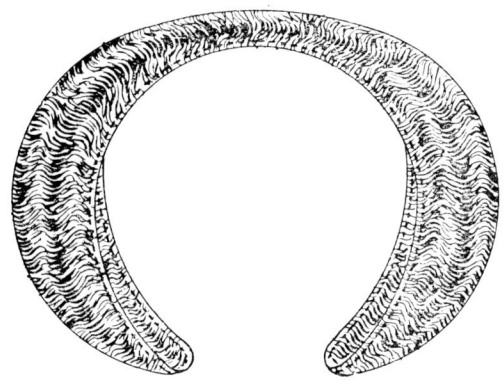

HD10311.—8¾d. each.

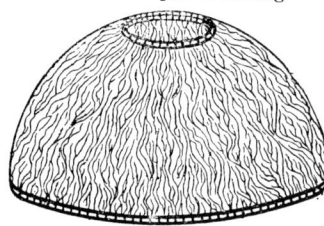

New Tournure Style, back frames for New Empire Dressing.

HD10312.—10¾d. each, with and without hole at side.

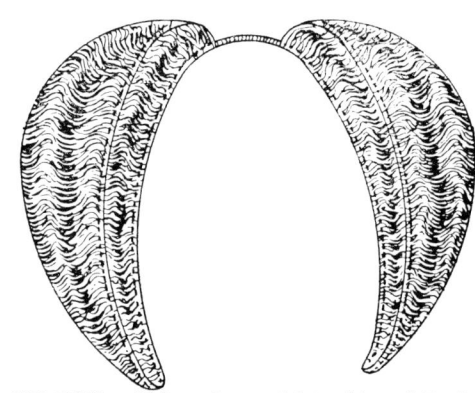

HD10313.—8¾d. each. Light, mid. and Dark Brown.

Wavy Hair Rolls.

HD10314.—18 in. 4¾d.

HD10315.—16 in. 4¾d.

HD10316.—12 in. 3¾d.

HD10317.—10 in. 2¾d.

These hair rolls are light, full and springy, and do not go hard or overheat the head.

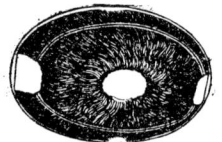

HD10319. Low, Curl Style Hair Frames, Gallon bound Edges, newest shape, 9¾d. each.

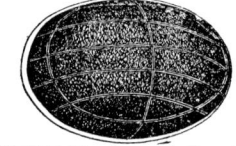

HD10322—Special line in Curl Frames, 4¾d. each.

HD10318.—14 in. 4¾d.

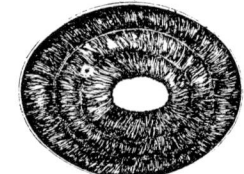

HD10323. — **New Curl Frame,** to Sketch. Colour, Light mid. and Dark Brown, 4¾d. each.

The KIN-CO SCARF CLIP, The new patent, enables one to arrange & securely fit Scarf in any Style. Simply press spring.

Can be had in Aluminium Gilt, Copper, Oxidised, Black, **1/-**

Also in better quality and imitation Tortoiseshell, **2/-**

HD10321.—6 in. 2¾d. pr

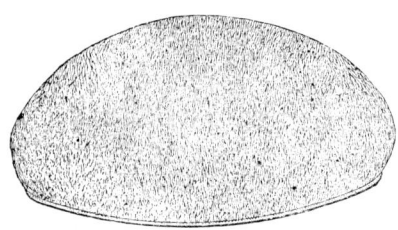

HD10320.—**Grecian or Curl Style Back Frames,** 6¾d. and 1/0¾ each, two qualities.

HD10324.— **New Tournure Style Back Frames** Best Wire and mohair covered Galloon, bound edges. Light mid. and Dark Brown, 10¾d. each.

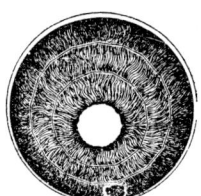

HD10325. — **Turban Shape Hair Frames,** to Sketch. 6¾d. each. Light mid. and Dark Brown.

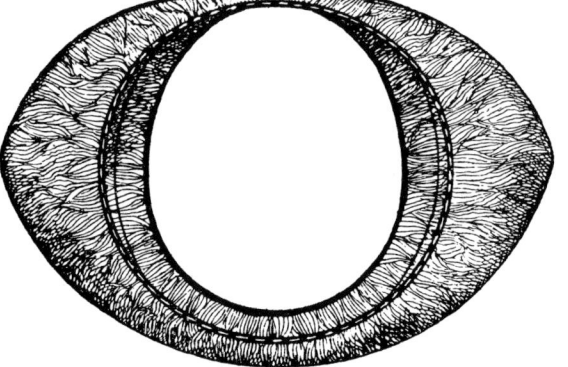

HD10326.—**All Round Full Dressing Frames,** Superior Quality, 1/6¾ each. Cheaper Quality, 1/0¾ each.

My lady in the hands of her maid.

Top left: A lady in the hands of her maid, 1904.
Mary Evans Picture Library

Above and left: Two mourning toques and a hat, the latter in grenadine and silk. These come from Bentalls' catalogue for 1912 and are priced about 13/11d. We are told that all mourning articles of dress could be made at very short notice. *P. Stevenson*

Left: The long 'hip subduing' corset of 1909. *P. Stevenson*

Below: The corset of 1903 giving the S bend stance. *P. Stevenson*

Above: The type of corset worn at the turn of the century, emphasising the hips, and high in the bust line. Worn over the chemise. *P. Stevenson*

Right: From 'Les Modes' c1908, a suspender belt worn over the corset with a strange type of brassière. This might be entitled 'Oh!' that this too, too solid flesh would melt'. *P. Stevenson*

Above: The corset of 1911 giving a top-heavy effect to the figure especially when wearing the huge hats of the period. Thick blue and white striped cotton knickers of this time.
P. Stevenson

FRANK BENTALL — KINGSTON ON THAMES
Phone—ONE P.O. Kingston. Private Exchange.

LADIES' UNDERSKIRTS—Continued.

Ten Examples of Value Giving Special Ranges of SATIN & CHIFFON TAFFETTA UNDERSKIRTS, all at keen competitive prices.

U4011. — Black and White **Moirette Underskirt**, in three different width stripes, and also in Light Grey and White Stripes, 4/11½ each, out size at 5/11½.

U4012. — Very smart Braided **Moirette Underskirt**, as sketch, thoroughly well made of good silk Moirette stocked in all colours, trimmed Russia Braid, 6/11½ each.

U4013. — A special Novelty, Black **Moirette Underskirt**, as sketch, Flounce relieved with White, Old Rose, Amethyst, Emerald, Censi, Royal and Grey stripes, Special Price, 4/11½

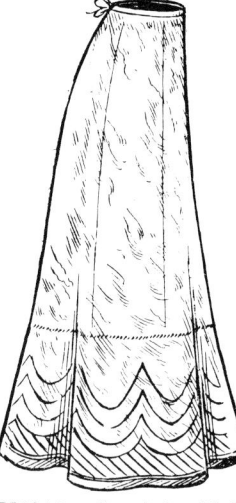

U4014.—Special **Moirette Underskirt**, with fancy band of White and Black stripe satinette at bottom. Stocked in all good shades and Black, 3/11¾ each.

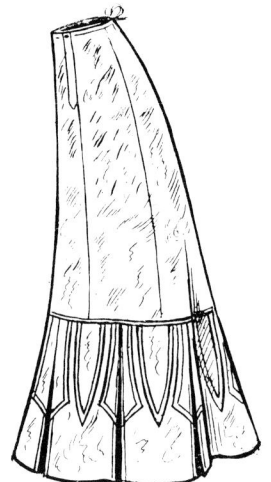

U4015. — Smart well finished **Moirette Underskirt**, nicely stitched flounce, stocked in all good shades, including, Greys, Art Blue, Old Rose, Amethyst, Browns, Navys and Blacks, 4/11½ each.

Special Range of Black Moirette Underskirts.
Stocked in Ordinary and Out Sizes.

No.	Price
1	3/11¾
2	4/11¾
3	5/11½
4	6/11½
5	8/11½
6	10/11
7	13/11
8	15/11
9	18/11

CARPETS.
Our New Extensive Showroom offers Greater Facilities for Business than hitherto.

Special Range of Black Satin Underskirts.
In Ordinary & Out Sizes.

No.	Price
S1	3/11¾ (Ordinary Size only)
S2	4/11½
S3	6/11½
S4	8/11½
S5	10/11
S6	13/11
S7	15/11
S8	21/11
S9	25/11

U4016.—White and Black Velvet Bound **Moirette Underskirt**, stocked in four designs, 3/11¾, also in out size, 4/9¾.

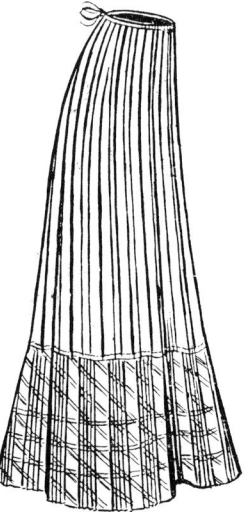

C4017. — Dainty silk finished **Moirette Underskirt**, smart design, as sketch, in all colours and Black, 6/11½.

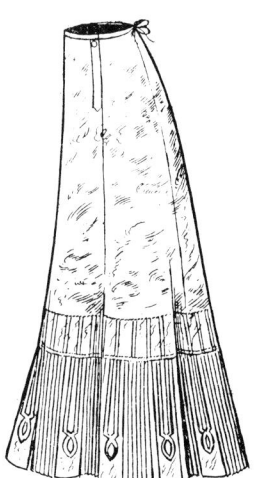

U4018.—Very Special Fine **Moirette Underskirt**, stocked in Art Blue, Quaker Grey, Amethyst, Old Rose, Durbar Brown Reseda, Bronze, Navy and Black, 5/11½ each.

U4019. — Black and White, and Grey and White Satin Stripe **Moirette Underskirt**, in six good designs, 6/11½ each, also in out sizes at 8/11½.

U4020.—Very Special Hard Wearing **Moreen Underskirt**, stocked in all colours and Black, 2/6¾ each. The value given here is exceptional.

IF YOU MOVE WITH THE TIMES, YOU'LL REMOVE WITH BENTALL'S.

FRANK BENTALL — 60 Separate Departments. — KINGSTON ON THAMES.

LADIES' UNDERSKIRTS. — JAPANESE SILK UNDERSKIRTS.
Continued.

U4211.—Smart **Princess Japanese Silk Washing Underskirt**, Flounce handsomely embroidered in exclusive design, and lined Nainsook for protection in wear, well cut and nicely finished. quoted at a very keen price, 17/11.

U4212.—Plain **Japanese Silk Princess Underskirt**, neatly pleated Flounce, well made and nicely finished. Special Price, 12/11.

U4213.—Dainty Washing **Japanese Princess Silk Underskirt**, trimmed at Bust with good Valenciennes lace and insertion, with four rows of insertion and lace at Flounce, and band of Satin Ribbon round top. Special Price 26/11. This skirt has an under flounce of Japanese silk protecting the lace.

U4214.—Elaborate **Japanese Silk Underskirt** handsomely trimmed with valenciennes lace and insertion. Deep protecting underflounce. Special Price, 21/11.

U4215.—Good quality **Japanese Silk Princess Underskirt**, Millanese Top to fit any figure, handsomely embroidered flounce, cut and finished in best possible manner, 23/11.

U4216.—Very Special elaborate **Washing Japanese Princess Silk Underskirt**, handsomely embroidered on bust as sketch, with 8 embroidered lapels at Flounce. Special Price, 21/11. Extreme Good Value.

U4217.—Exclusive **Washing Japanese Princess Silk Underskirt**, very smart and effective design, Millanese Top to fit any figure, handsomely embroidered as sketch, 29/11.

U4218. — Ordinary **Japanese Silk Underskirt**, trimmed valenciennes lace and insertion, with protecting underflounce. Very Special Price, 10/11.

U4219.—Dainty **Japanese Silk Underskirt**, trimmed valenciennes lace with protecting underflounce. Special Price, 13/11.

LADIES' UNDERCLOTHING.

Selected Group of Ladies' Lingerie.
All Garments to match.

UC1.—Handmade Longcloth Nightdress, trimmed good Embroidery & Insertion, fine Tucks and Feathering. Our Leading Line, 4/11½.

UC2.—Nainsook Nightdress, square neck, trimmed good Swiss Embroidery and Insertion, 3/11¾.
Combinations to match, 3/11¾.
Chemise   ,,   ,,   2/11¾.
Knickers   ,,   ,,   1/11¾.
Camisole   ,,   ,,   1/11¾.

UC3.—Hand Sewn Nainsook Nightdress, effectively trimmed Val. Lace and Insertion and Finely Tucked, 8/11½.

UC4.—Nainsook Nightdress, Pretty Yoke of Torchon Lace and Cambric Insertion. Splendid Value, 3/11¾.

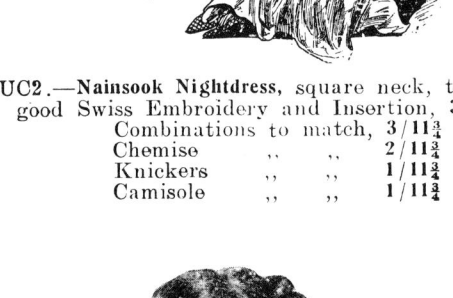

UC5.—Longcloth Nightdress, trimmed Embroidery and Insertion and Ribbon Insertion. Good Value, 2/11¾.

UC6.—Nainsook Nightdress, very Smart Design, trimmed Cluny Lace and Insertion, 3/11¾.

UC7.—Dainty Nainsook Nightdress, trimmed Smart Swiss Insertion and Fine Valenciennes Lace and Insertion, threaded ribbon, 7/11½.

UC8.—Nainsook Nightdress, effectively trimmed wide Ribbon Insertion and Fine Torchon Lace, 5/11½.

LADIES' UNDERCLOTHING—Continued.
Smart designs in Ladies' Lingerie Daintily trimmed Lace and Embroidery.

UC9.—**Longcloth Combinations**, trimmed Embroidery and Insertion, threaded Ribbon. Smart Shape, 2/11¾.

UC11.—**Good Long-cloth Combinations**, trimmed Embroidery and Insertion and fine tucks. 4/11½.

UC10.—**Nainsook Nightdress.** Square Neck. Trimmed Torchon Lace and Insertion, 4/11½. Ditto with Collar, 4/6½.
Combinations to match, 3/11¾. Knickers to match, 2/11¾.
Chemises ,, ,, 2/11¾. Camisoles ,, ,, 2/6¼.

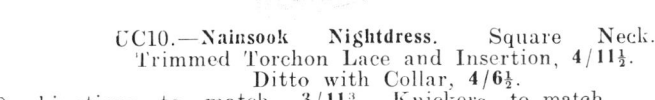

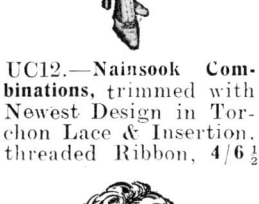

UC12.—**Nainsook Combinations**, trimmed with Newest Design in Torchon Lace & Insertion, threaded Ribbon, 4/6½.

UC13.—**Ribbon waist, Combinations** smartly trimmed Torchon Lace. Good shape, 6/11½.

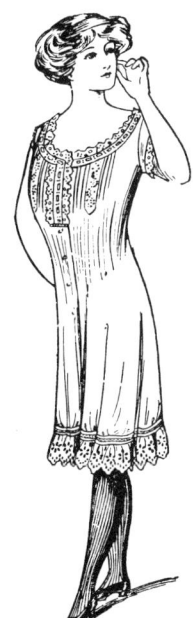

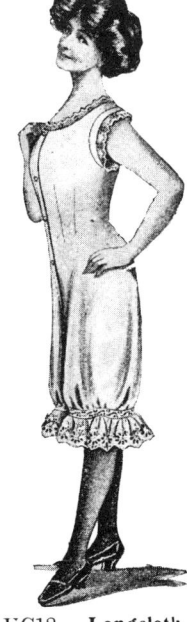

UC14. Nainsook Camisole Elaborately trimmed Torchon Lace and Insertion. With Puff Sleeves, 1/11¾.

UC15.—**Nainsook Combinations**, Prettily trimmed Lace and Insertion and Fancy Braid Insertion, 3/11¾.

UC16.—**Longcloth Combinations**, (Special Value). Trimmed Embroidery and Insertion, 2/6¼.

UC17.—**Nainsook Combinations**, Effectively trimmed Lace & Insertion, Splendid Value, 2/11¾.

UC18.—**Longcloth Combinations**, Trimmed Embroidery. Good Value, 1/11¾.

UC19.—**Pretty Camisole**, trimmed Cluny Torchon Lace and Insertion, threaded Ribbon, 1/11¾.

FRANK BENTALL — Removals & Warehousing. — Kingston on Thames

LADIES' UNDERCLOTHING—continued.
Charming Styles in Chemises and Knickers, prettily trimmed Lace and Embroidery.

UC34. Nainsook Chemise, Very Pretty Design, trimmed Val. Lace and Insertion, threaded ribbon, 2/11¾

UC35.—Nainsook Chemise, trimmed Valenciennes Lace and Embroidery and Lace Insertion. Special Value, 1/11¾

UC36. Nainsook Knickers, *New Elastic Waist*, prettily trimmed Val. Lace and Insertion. 2/11¾

UC37.—Nainsook Chemise, Very Handsome Yoke of Maltese Lace and Swiss Insertion, 3/11¾

UC38.—Dainty Chemise, Nainsook, trimmed Fine Torchon Lace and Effective Ribbon Insertion, 4/6¼

UC39.—Longcloth Knickers, trimmed Strong Embroidery, 1/6¾

UC40. Longcloth Chemise, good shape, trimmed Embroidery & Insertion and Fine Tucks, 1/11¾

UC41.—New Design Nainsook Chemise, trimmed Choice Swiss Embroidery and Insertion, threaded Ribbon, 3/11¾

UC42. Longcloth Knickers, trimmed Very Effective Embroidery & Insertions, Good Patterns, 1/11¾

UC43.—Longcloth Chemise, Trimmed Embroidery and Insertion, 1/6¾

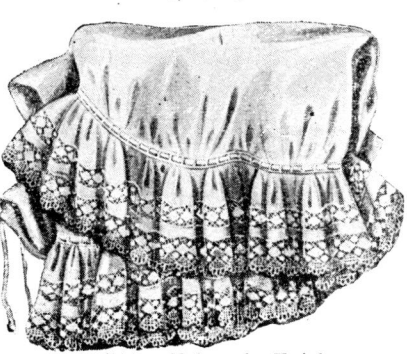

UC44.—Nainsook Knickers, effectively trimmed Torchon Lace & Insertion, wide knees. (Special Line), 1/11¾

UC45. Nainsook Chemise, trimmed Fine Torchon Lace and Insertion. (New Pattern). Threaded Ribbon, 2/11¾

UC46.—Nainsook Chemise, effective Yoke, square shape, trimmed Swiss Insertion and Torchon Lace and Insertion, 2/9¾

FRANK BENTALL — 60 Separate Departments. — Kingston on Thames.

LADIES' UNDERCLOTHING—*continued.*

Camisoles.

Dainty and Irresistible Designs at convincing Prices.

UC20. Nainsook, trimmed Strong Lace & Insertion & Tucks, 1/6¾

UC21.—Camisole, with Puff Sleeve, trimmed Fine Lace & Insertion & Appliques, 2/11¾

UC22.—Nainsook Camisole, trimmed Lace and Insertion. Our Price, 1/0¾

UC23.—Camisole, High Neck, Puff Sleeves, Val. Lace and Insertion Yoke, 2/11¾

UC24. Nainsook Camisole, very Pretty Yoke and Puff Sleeve, trimmed Val. Lace & Insertion, 2/11¾

UC25.—Nainsook Camisole, Pretty Design, trimmed Swiss and Torchon Insertion, edged Torchon Lace. Special Value, 1/11¾

UC26.—Nainsook Camisole, very effective Yoke with Ribbon and Lace & Insertion and edged Lace, 2/11¾

UC27. Nainsook Camisole, Puff Sleeves and finely tucked at waist, trimmed Torchon Lace and Insertion, 2/9¾

UC28.—Nainsook, trimmed Val. lace & Insertion & Swiss Motifs, 2/6¾

UC29.—Pretty Camisole, trimmed Val. Lace and Insertion and Cambric Insertion, 2/9¾

UC30.—Camisole, High Neck, Very Effective Lace and Insertion Yoke, Good Value, 1/11¾

UC31.—Nainsook Camisole, trimmed Torchon Lace & fine Swiss Insertion, 1/11¾

UC32.—Nainsook Camisole, Pretty Lace Yoke Threaded Ribbon. Special Price, 1/11¾

UC33.—Pretty Camisole, trimmed Maltese Lace and Insertion & Swiss Ribbon Insertion, 3/11¾

FRANK BENTALL — Removals & Warehousing — KINGSTON ON THAMES

LADIES' UNDERCLOTHING—*continued*.

New Designs in Ladies' Nightdresses, Combinations and Chemises.

U5211. — Longcloth Nightdress, turn-down collar, trimmed Embroidery & Insertion. Good value. Price 2/11¾.

U5212. — Empire Style Longcloth Nightdress. Yoke of good Embroidery Insertion. Price 6/11½.

U5213. — Longcloth Nightdress, good useful style, Collar trimmed Embroidery also down front with small tucks. Price 3/11¾.

U5214 — Longcloth Chemise, smart yoke of Embroidery Anglaise edged narrow Embroidery. Price 1/11¾.

U5215. — Good Strong Longcloth Combinations, trimmed Embroidery and feathering. Price 1/11¾.

U5216. — New Design, Nainsook Chemise, Empire style, trimmed Lace and Beading, threaded Ribbon. Price 3/11¾.

U5217. — Useful Combinations, trimmed Embroidery, Tucked knee band, two frills of Embroidery. Special Value, Price 3/11¾.

U5218. — Hand Sewn Longcloth Nightdress, trimmed Embroidery and Insertion and Fine Tucks. Price 6/11½.

U5219. — Nainsook Nightdress, Empire neck, smart yoke of Embroidery, Insertion and Beading threaded ribbon. Price 4/11½.

U5220. — Longcloth Combinations, good quality cloth, trimmed blind Embroidery and Tucked knee band. Price 3/11¾.

FRANK BENTALL

Write, Call or Phone.   KINGSTON ON THAMES.

LADIES' UNDERCLOTHING—*continued.*

Dainty Knickers Chemises and Camisoles, Newest Designs

U5311.—Longcloth Knickers, trimmed good embroidery and insertion. Price 1/11¾

U5312.—Dainty and Useful Embroidery Camisole, High Neck, three-quarter sleeve. Price 2/9¾

U5313.—Special Line, Smart Camisole, with lace yoke. Price 1/0¾

U5314.—Longcloth Knickers, trimmed effective embroidery and feathering. Price 2/11¾

A GOOD ASSORTMENT OF HIGH NECK CAMISOLES WITH PUFF SLEEVES, 1/6¾, 1/11¾, 2/6¾, 2/11¾.

"OUTSIZE GARMENTS," CHEMISES, KNICKERS, COMBINATIONS, CAMISOLES, NIGHTDRESSES, ETC., ALWAYS OBTAINABLE AT OUR STORE.

ALL READY TO WEAR GARMENTS AT BENTALL'S BARGAIN PRICES.

LADIES' BUST BODICES AND BUST IMPROVERS, Price, 1/11¾, 2/11¾, 3/6¾

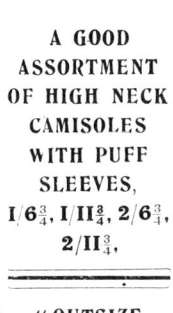

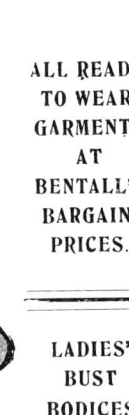
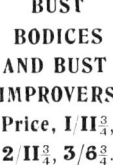

U5315.—Camisole with puff sleeves, prettily trimmed lace and insertion. Good shape. Price 1/9¾

U5316.—Pretty Camisole, effective yoke and puff sleeve of lace. Price 1/11¼

U5317.—Nainsook Chemises, trimmed lace and insertion, exceedingly effective style. Special price, 1/11¼

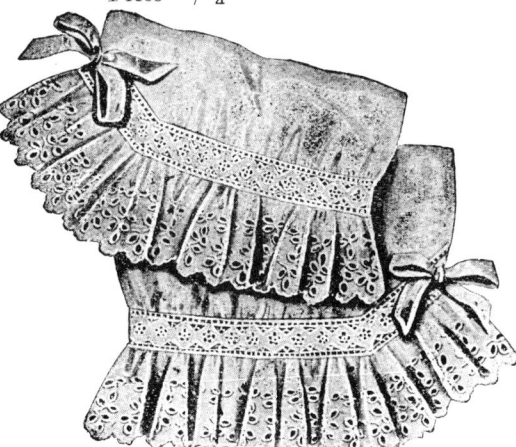

U5318.—Smart Knickers, French knee, trimmed good pattern embroidery and insertion and ribbon bow. Price 2/6¾

U5319.—Good Strong Longcloth Chemises, with tucks and insertion down front, edged embroidery. Price 2/6¾

U5320.—Dainty Nainsook Knickers, lace trimmed, wide knee, threaded ribbon. Price 1/11¾

W.B. Reduso Corsets

W.B. Hip-Subduing. No. 121.
A splendid model for average or well developed figures, has the specially constructed abdominal support clasp, the bust and under arm is low, while the hips and back are long. It is made of strong Coutil in White and Grey, trimmed at the top with embroidery, and has suspenders at front and side. Sizes 18 to 30 ins. **Price 6/11**

No. 368. Exactly the same shape as No. 121, but is made from a new design of French Broche, in White-Sky only. Trimmed with embroidery to match, and has suspenders at front and side. Sizes 18 to 30 ins. **Price 12/11**

W.B. Reduso Corsets, shape the large figure into graceful proportions, and reduces hips and abdomen from ONE TO FIVE INCHES, without straps or other injurious attachment. They are also delightfully comfortable.

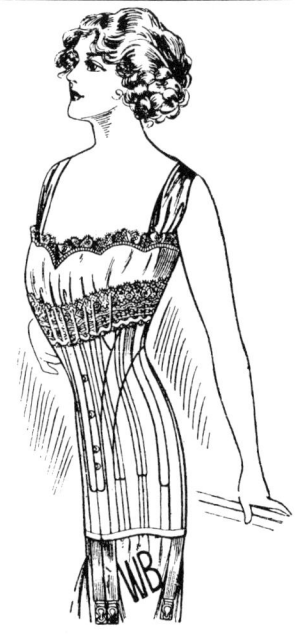

W.B. Nuform. No. 363.
A new long model for average figures at a popular price. Made from strong Coutil in White and Grey, low from the waist line up, and long over the hips and back. Trimmed with lace and has suspenders at front and sides. Sizes 18 to 30 ins. **Price 2/11**

W.B. Hip-Subduing. No. 759.
A very popular model. The material is Coutil in White, Ecru, and Grey. It is trimmed at the top with a band of satin ribbon edged with lace. Hose supporters both at front and sides. Size 18 to 30 ins. **Price 6/11**
W.B. Nuform: No. 765.
Is the same Model, but the material is Batiste in White only. It is trimmed at the top with binding of Batiste and lace. Hose supporters at front and sides. Sizes 18 to 26 ins. **Price 3/11**

W.B. Reduso Corsets No. 772.

A Perfect Corset for large women. It is scientifically constructed, and positively ensures a reduction of the over developed parts from one inch to five inches, thus giving the stout women the graceful lines of their more slender sisters. Made of durable White, Ecru, and Grey Coutil, and daintily trimmed at the top with lace and baby ribbon, finished with a satin bow. The bust is medium in height, with the necessary length over and around the hips. Four hose supporters attached to the front and two at the sides. Sizes 20 to 36 ins. **Price 12/11**

. . DON'T WAIT . .
COME AND BE FITTED NOW.

W.B. Nuform. No. 477.
A Model with long subdued hips and abdomen lines for average figures. Modelled like a girdle above the waist, it is very low in the bust and under arms. Made of a substantial Coutil in White and Grey, lace trimmed. Hose supporters at front and sides. Sizes 18 to 30 ins. **Price 3/11**

Ladies walking by the Seine. These dresses owed their extraordinary shape to the corsets underneath. *P. Stevenson*

FRANK BENTALL — Surrey's Premier Store. — KINGSTON ON THAMES.

HOSIERY DEPARTMENT.

H9611. — **Navy Cotton Hose**, assorted Vertical Stripes, 6¾d. pair to sketch.

H9612. — **Black Cotton and Wool Hose**, Vertical Stripes, White, Sky, Pink, Heliotrope 1/0¾ pair to sketch.

H9613.—**Ladies' Mercerised Lisle Thread Hose**, Lace Ankle, 1/0¾ pair to sketch, colours: Grey, Mole, Reseda, Purple Light and Dark Saxe.

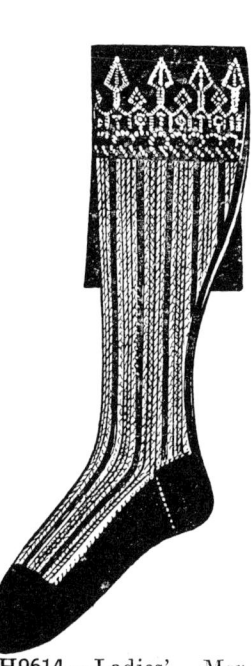

H9614.—**Ladies' Mercerised Black Lisle Hose**, Lace Ankles, 1/0¾ pair.

H9615.—**Black Cotton and Wool Hose**, Vertical Stripes; Colours: White, Sky, Pink, Heliotrope, 1/0¾ pair to sketch.

Every line here represents Best Value.

Removals at Economy Prices

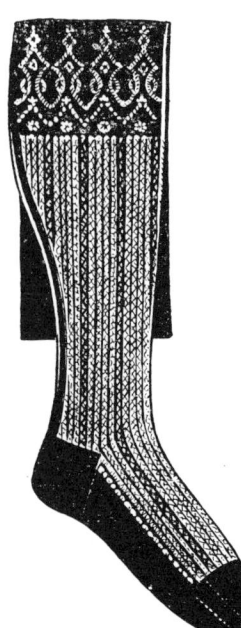

H9616. — **Ladies' Lisle Hose**, Lace Ankles, Tan and Black 9¾d. pair, exact to sketch.

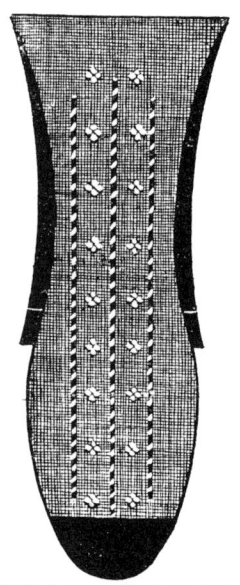

H9617. — **Black Cashmere Finish Hose**, Vertical Fronts, embroidered Purple and White; Sky and White; Green and White; Black and White; Pink and White; 1/4¾ pair.

H9618.—**Black Cotton Hose**, Fancy Vertical Stripes, White, Sky, Pink, Reseda, Purple, 6¾d. pair to sketch.

H9619.—**Black Cashmere Finish Hose**, Vertical Fronts, Black, White, and Green; Black, Pink and Green; Black, White and Sky; Black, Sky and Pink; Black, Pink and White; Black, Green and Sky; 1/4¾ pair to sketch.

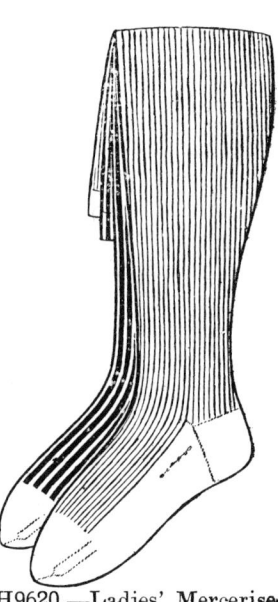

H9620.—**Ladies' Mercerised drop thread Lisle Hose**, 1/0¾ pair; Colours: Light and Dark Saxe, Grey, Reseda, Mole, Amethyst.

FRANK BENTALL — LUNCHEON AND TEA ROOM FIRST FLOOR — KINGSTON ON THAMES.

HOSIERY DEPARTMENT—*Continued*.

H9711.—**Grey Cotton Hose**, Vertical Stripes, to sketch, 6¾d. per pair.

H9712.—**Black Cashmere Hose**, Vertical Stripes, White, Sky, Pink, Heliotrope, Green 1/4¾ pair to sketch.

H9713.—**Ladies' Black & Coloured Cashmere Hose**, Vertical Stripes, Embroidered Self, Sky, Heliotrope, Green and White 1/11¾.

H9714.—**Ladies' Black Lisle Finish Hose**, wide double tops, high spliced heel, double sole, 6¾d. pair.

H9715.—Coloured Lisle Mercerised Hose, Vertical Open Stitch 10¾d. pair, all colours.

H9716.—**Black Cashmere Finish Hose**, Vertical Stripes, White, Sky, Pink and Green, 1/0¾ pair to sketch.

H9717.—**Black Cotton & Wool Hose**, Vertical Stripes, White, Sky, Pink, Heliotrope, 1/0¾ to sketch.

NEW EXTENSIONS
Enables us to give better selection and value.

Order by Post with Confidence. This list will help you.

H9719.—**Ladies' Black Cotton Hose**, natural feet, spliced heels and toes, stainless dye, 6¾d. per pair.

H9720.—**Coloured Lisle Hose**, best Silk finish, Vertical open stitch, 1/4¾ pair, all colours.

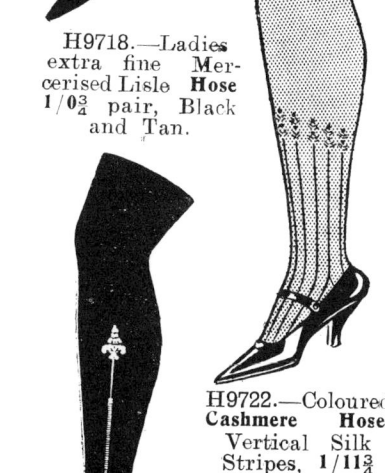

H9718.—Ladies extra fine Mercerised Lisle Hose 1/0¾ pair, Black and Tan.

H9721.—**Ladies' Black Cotton Hose**, embroidered; Coloured Clox Stainless Dye 6¾d. pair.

H9722.—Coloured **Cashmere Hose**, Vertical Silk Stripes, 1/11¾ pair; Colours: Amethyst, Green, Grey, Saxe, Mole, Purple. To Sketch.

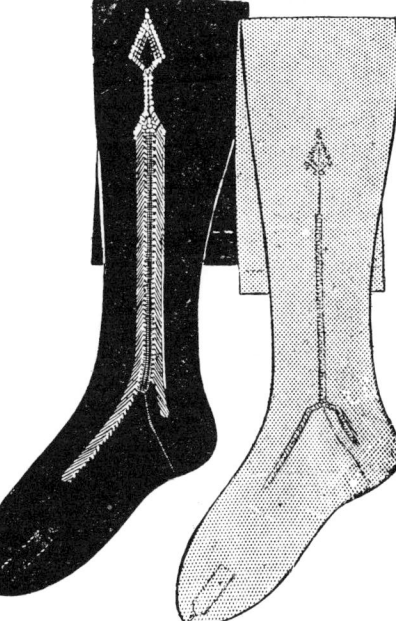

H9723.—**Ladies' Black Lisle Hose**, Lace Clox, 10¾d. pair, exact to sketch.

H9724.—**Ladies' Coloured Cotton Hose**, embroidered self Clox, 6¾d. pair. Colours: Grey, Mole, Saxe, Green and Amethyst.

Children

Above left: Tea in the garden at Exeter in the late 1890s.

Left: A proud mother of a large family! Dora and her dolls c1895.

Top: A little brother and sister. Colin and Christine Ellis c1897.

Top right: Sybil Jerman aged 13 in 1898. Note the pinafore and straw hat.

Right: Two sisters and their twin brothers. The elder in a light dress and black stockings and shoes; the boys with waistcoats and watchchains, about 1898.

Above: Unsuitably dressed at the seaside in 1899.

Above: Confirmation dresses from an old photograph in a family album dated c1900. *P. Stevenson*

Above right: A very similar type of confirmation dress worn by Lady Helen Windsor, daughter of the Duke and Duchess of Kent, at her comfirmation in April 1978. *P. Stevenson*

Right: A nurse and her charge about 1900.

Far right: Mother, nurse and baby, 1900.

Left: Eryk and Margaret Evans in 1900. Although the boy's hair is cut short and he wears a sailor hat, his coat is like a girl's. She is carrying a large muslin and lace-trimmed hat.

Right: A little girl in a white muslin and lace trimmed dress about 1900.

Below right: A typical outdoor coat and bonnet for a small child in 1900.

Bottom right: Sybil Jerman in 1900 aged 15. The hair is still worn long but the blouse looks very 'grown-up'.

Right: One of four small bridesmaids at the wedding in 1900 of Earl Granville to Miss Nina Baring. They wore long Empire-style trained frocks of white satin with square necks and tiny sleeves and frilled chiffon fichus knotted in front. Pale blue sashes were tied under the left arm with a bow and with long ends falling to the hem. They wore soft hats of white muslin with tucked frills round the brim which were trimmed with large soft blue satin bows to match the dresses. Their gloves were of white kid, and their shoes of white satin. The bridegroom's gift to each was an enamelled heart-shaped brooch set with diamonds and pearls. *P. Stevenson*

Left: Baby's christening robe showing Indian motifs. *P. Stevenson*

CHILDREN LOVE... JERSEYS!

They can play in them— Nuthin' to spoil.

"Two Steeples" Regd.

Every Garment Guaranteed

Comfy and Warm. Free and Easy.

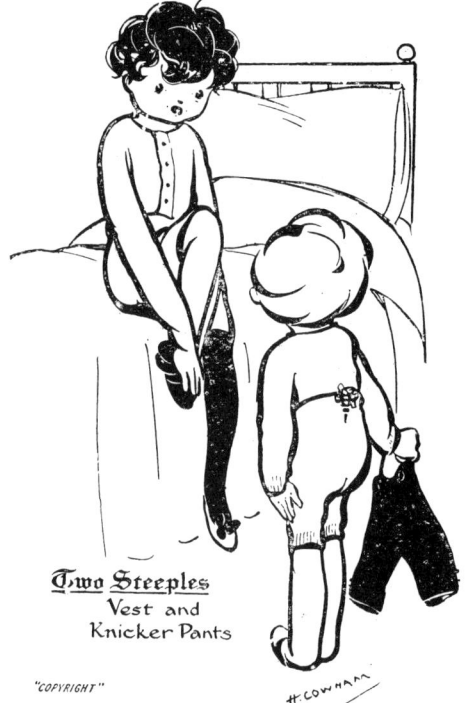

Two Steeples Vest and Knicker Pants

UC2.—**Ladies Nightdresses**, Tropica Cotton Aermagna. Price, 4/11½. Also in Girls, Maids, and Large Maids. 4/6½, 4/9½, 4/11½.

Two Steeples Sleeping Suits

UC1.—**Vests and Knicker Pants**. Every Garment Guaranteed, whether made of Pure Wool, Cotton and Wool, or Pure Cotton, for Washing and Wearing. Prices, Pure Wool Vests from 2/11, according to size. Knicker Pants, 3/6, according to size. "Air" Fabric Vests or Knicker Pants from 2/6, according to size.

UC3.—"**The Little Ones' Night Comforts**." Sleeping Suits, Pure Wool, Winter Weight, Natural and White. No Feet. Sizes 1 5/6½, 2 5/9½, 3 5/11½, 4 6/3½. With Feet. Sizes 1 6/6½, 2 6/9½, 3 6/11½, 4 7/3½.

Ditto Merino Natural, and White.

No Feet. Sizes 1 2/6¾, 2 2/9¾, 3 2/11¾, 4 3/3¾, 5 3/6¾. With Feet. Sizes 1 3/6¾, 2 3/9¾, 3 3/11¾, 4 4/3½, 5 4/6½.

Two Steeples Jersey Boy

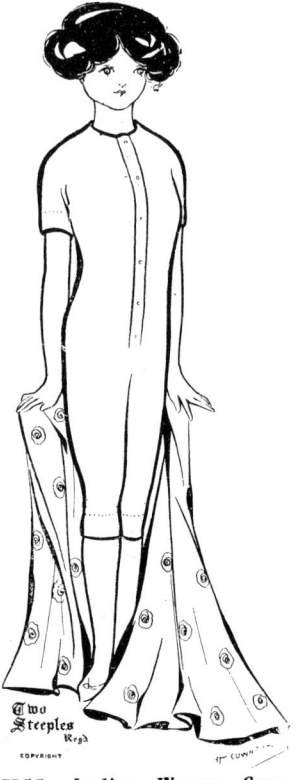

Two Steeples

Two Steeples Jersey Girl

UC4.—**Pure Wool "Jersey Suits,"** Wash and Wear like Linen, made in the following Art Shades, Reseda, Tan, Cream, Cardinal, Navy, Dk. Saxe, and Arctic Blue, in sizes 18 5/11½, 20 6/6½, 22 6/11½, 24 7/6½. Caps to match, 1/- extra.

UC5.—**Ladies Woven Combinations**, Natural and White all Wool. S.W. 5/11½, W. 5/11½, O.S. 6/11½, High Neck, Short Sleeves. Merino, 3/11¾, 3/11½, 4/6½.

UC6.—**Girls Kilt Suits**. All wool unshrinkable, in cream, Tan, Navy, Arctic Blue Dk. Saxe, Reseda. Sizes 19½ 7/11½, 20½ 8/3½, 23½ 8/11½, 25½ 9/6½, 27½ 9/11½.

Right: From 'Les Modes' 1901 and called 'Robe pour Baby' and said to be from 'an English warehouse'. It is composed of a silk pleated skirt with a chiffon and lace bodice surmounted by a satin bolero trimmed with ribbon rouleau knots. The incredible hat is not described. Someone has put rings and bracelets on the poor child and stuffed tiger lilies into her hot little hand. *P. Stevenson*

Below: Children's costumes in the illustrations by H. R. Millar in the *Strand Magazine* for E. Nesbit's story 'The Phoenix and the Carpet'. *Ernest Benn Ltd*

Left: This shows the strange fashion of dressing little boys as girls even to the length of curling their long hair and tying it up with ribbon bows. This is remarkable when contrasted with the extreme masculinity of older boys' fashions; c1902. *P. Stevenson*

Left: The wide use of the apron, the straw hat and a practical small boy's dress c1903. *P. Stevenson*

Above: Dora Jerman about 1903 in a dress made for her by her mother for her dancing class. It was of cherry red cashmere with an écru lace collar.

Right: A schoolgirl c1902. Note the light dress with watch-pocket in waist belt, high neck, gloves, black shoes and stockings. The dress is made with tucks to allow for growth. *P. Stevenson*

JUVENILE DEPARTMENT.

J1911.—27/6.
Smart **Coat and Skirt** for Young Ladies in Navy Blue and Coloured Serge. Sizes 7, 8 and 9.

J1912.—12/11 Size 4. Rise **1/3** each size.
Girl's **Coat and Skirt** made in Navy and Coloured Serge. ¾ length skirt. Sizes 4 to 9.

LARGE ASSORTMENT OF COSTUMES, FROCKS, PALETOTS, ETC., FOR YOUNG LADIES WEAR AT SPECIAL PRICES.

J1913.—18/11.
Young Ladies **Costume**, in good quality Serge. Smartly Tailored in Navy, Grey and Amethyst.

J1914.—25/9.
Very useful **Costume** for Young Ladies in Striped Tweed, Light and Dark Greys and other Colours. Sizes 7, 8 and 9.

OUR NEW JUVENILE DEPARTMENT IS NOW OPEN.

GIRLS' MACINTOSHES AND CRAVENETTE RAIN COATS IN ALL SIZES.

J1915.—12/11 for 33 in. Rise **1/0** each size.
Girl's **Paletot**, in Summer Serge, Navy, Grey, Saxe, Amethyst and Cream. Special Value.

J1916.—25/9.
Smart **Costume** for Young Ladies in Serge, all Colours, trimmed contrasting shades. Sizes 7, 8 and 9.

FRANK BENTALL — Write, Call or Phone. — KINGSTON ON THAMES.

CHILDREN'S OUTFITTING DEPARTMENT—Continued.

A HUGE STOCK OF WOOL GOODS ON HAND TO SELECT FROM.

C6611.—**Girls' Sports Coat**, Cream and exceedingly smart shape, Price **18/11**

C6612.—**Infants' Knitted Wool Overalls.**
Size 1 2 3 4
1/4¾ 1/6¾ 1/9¾ 1/11¾
Also in Hand Knitted (Fancy Stitch).
1/11¾ 2/6¾ 2/11¾ 3/6¾

C6613.—**Infants' Wool Drawers**, Machine made.
Size 1 2 3 4
1/0¾ 1/2¾ 1/4¾ 1/6¾

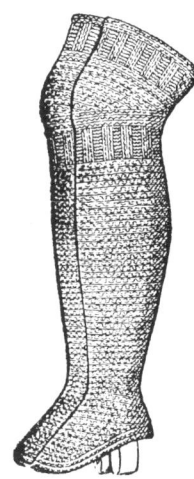

C6614.—**Children's Knitted Wool Gaiters.**
Size 1 2 3 4
6¾d. 8¾d. 10¾d. 1/0¾
Also better quality.
1/0¾ 1/2¾ 1/4¾ 1/6¾

C6615.—**Children's Cream Knitted Wool Coats.** New Style.
18 in. 20 in. 22 in. 24 in.
10/6 11/9 12/11 13/11

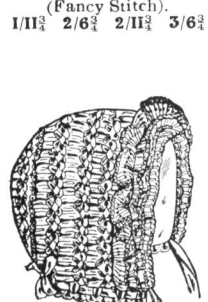

C6617.—**Infant's Hand Knitted Wool Hood.**
1/11¾ and 2/11¾

C6620.—**Infants' Shoes.** Lamb skin. Natural form. Soft soles. Ankle strap. In White or Tan.
Size 2 3 4
1/2¾ 1/3¾ 1/4¾

C6622.—**Knitted Slouch Hat** in Cream. Price **9¾d.**

C6618.—**Infants' White Wool Boots.** Hand made.
1/0¾ Also Machine made Boots, 4¾d., 6¾d., 8¾d., and 10¾d.

C6619.—**New Overall Gaiter.** In Cream, Tan and Navy Stockinette.
Size 1 2 3
1/9½ 1/11¾ 2/3¾

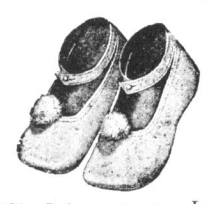

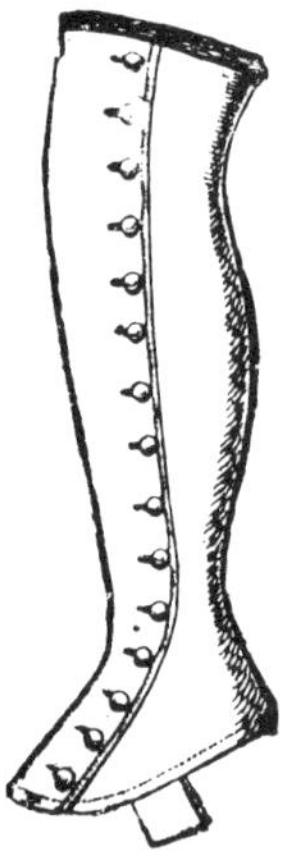

C6616.—**Children's Stockinette Gaiters.**
Size 1 2 3 4
1/6¾ 1/9¾ 1/11¾ 2/3¾
In Navy, Tan, Cream, Cardinal and Beaver. Quality cheaper.
1/0¾ 1/2¾ 1/4¾ 1/6¾

C6621.—**Infants' Wool Jackets.** Cream only.
Sizes 1 2 3
1/9¾ 1/11¾ 2/3¾

C6623.—**Infants' Moccasins** in White and Tan.
Size 1 2
1/11¾ 1/11¾

C6624.—**Wool Polo Caps,** similar to sketch. In all Colours. **1/0¾**
Cheaper qualities, 6¾d., 8¾d. and 10¾d.

C6625.—**Infants' White Wool Boots,** Viyella.
6¾d., 8¾d. and 1/0¾

C6626.—**Childs' Wool Hood.** White, Reseda, Saxe, Navy, Brown, Cardinal. Price **1/0¾**

C6627.—**White Wool Infantees.**
3¾d. 4¾d.
6¾d. 8d.
10¾d. 1/0¾

C6628.—**Infants' Wrapper Vests.** All Wool. Short sleeves.
1 2 3 4
1/0¾ 1/2¾ 1/4¾ 1/6¾
Long sleeves.
1/3¾ 1/4¾ 1/6¾ 1/9¾

C6629.—**Infants' Jerseys in Cream.**
Size 1 2/3¾; size 2, 2/6¾

FRANK BENTALL

Phone—ONE P.O. Kingston. Private Exchange.

Kingston on Thames.

CHILDREN'S OUTFITTING DEPARTMENT—Continued.

Dainty Frocks, etc., for the Mites.

F6711.—**A Charming Muslin Frock.** Trimmed Embroidery, and Threaded Ribbon. Pretty Long-Waisted Style. 19 in., **8/11½**, 21 in., **9/11½**, 23 in., **10/11**.

F6712.—**New Style, Silk Frock.** Trimmed Lace and Lace Insertions, and Hemstitching, very effective and becoming Style. 21 in., **8/11½**, 24 in., **10/11**, 27 in., **12/11**, 30 in., **14/11**, 33 in., **16/11**, 36 in., **18/11**.

F6713.—**Pretty Style, White Muslin Frock.** Trimmed imitation Val Lace Threaded Ribbon at Waist. 19 in., **8/11½**, 21 in., **9/11½**, 23 in., **10/11**.

F6714.—**Dainty Muslin Frock.** Trimmed Embroidery and Valenciennes Lace Threaded Ribbon. 19 in., **6/11½**, 21 in., **7/6½**, 24 in., **7/11½**.

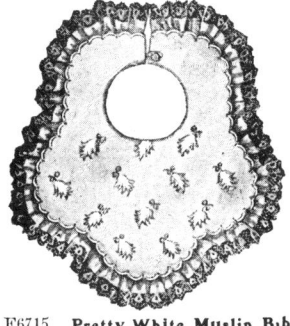

F6715.—**Pretty White Muslin Bib.** Trimmed Val. Lace. Price, **11¾**. Also similar Designs. Price, **1/0¾, 1/11¾**.

F6716.—**Childrens' Yokes.** White Muslin, and finely Embroidered. Price, **1/9¾**. Other very effective Designs, **10¾, 1/0¾, 1/3¾, 1/6¾, 1/11¾, 2/11¾**.

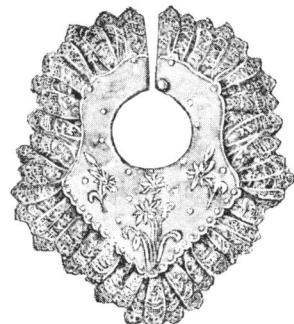

F6717.—**Infants' Bibs.** Effective Designs, Trimmed Embroidery. Price, **8¾, 1/0¾, 1/3¾, 1/6¾**.

F6718.—**Infants' Muslin Frocks.** Trimmed Imitation Val. Lace and Ribbon. 18 in. and 20 in. Price, **4/11½**.

F6719.—**Infants' Frocks.** Empire Style, Embroidered Muslin, Yoke and Sleeves, Threaded Ribbon, one size only, **7/11½**.

F6720.—**Baby Hair Brush** in White, Pink, and Sky, Price, **1/0¾**. Plain Back, Ditto. Price, **10¾**.

F6723.—**Powder Box.** Inlaid "Baby," Pink, White, and Sky. Price, **10¾**.

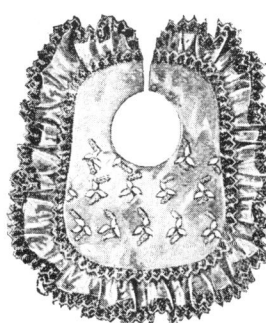

F6721.—**Dainty Silk Bibs** Embroidered and Edge Lace. Very pretty Designs. Price, **1/3¾, 1/6¾, 1/11¾**.

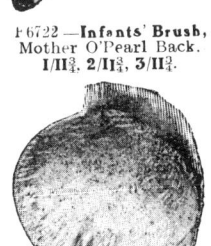

F6722.—**Infants' Brush,** Mother O'Pearl Back. **1/11¾, 2/11¾, 3/11¾**.

F6724.—**Powder Puffs.** Various Sizes. **4¾, 6¾, 8¾, 10¾, 1/0¾**.

F6725.—**Powder Box,** useful Size, Pink, Sky, and White. Price, **1/0¾, and 1/4¾**.

If you MOVE with the Times, You'll REMOVE with BENTALL'S.

Top right: Colin Ellis on his pony, 1903.

Right: A family group in the garden, 1904.

Below right: A growing informality in children's clothing is shown in this family group. The mother was an ardent suffragette.

Below: Little boy in a linen dress with large tucks, bare feet and sandals, 1906.

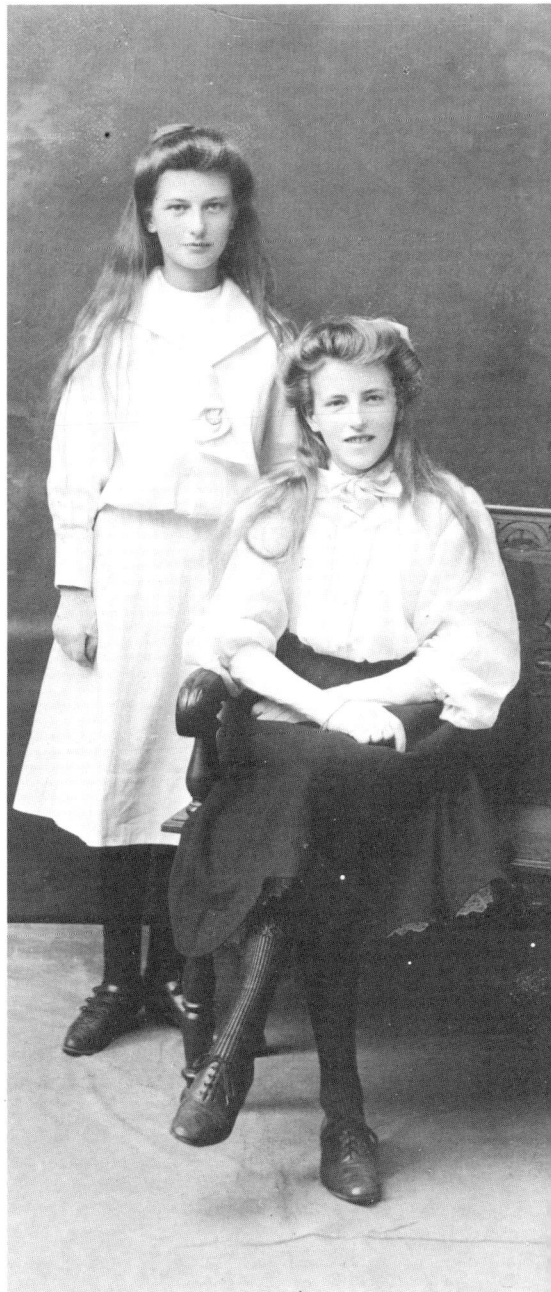

Above: A young girl about 16 in 1904 posed in the style of the currently popular sentimental postcards.

Above right: Teenagers about 14-years old in 1906. Note the sailor-style blouse, long white gloves and hint of frilly petticoat, black stockings and shoes.

Right: On the sands at Broadstairs in 1907.

Top left: A beautifully pleated dress for a small girl in 1907.

Above: Ethel Ellis (née Clarke) with her beloved doll, Eve, in 1907. Eve was an ardent Tory, hence the rosette.

Left: This family group about 1907 shows the ever-popular blouse, the little girl in embroidered muslin and the stiff collar and cuffs and laced boots worn by men of the period.

CHILDREN'S DEPARTMENT.

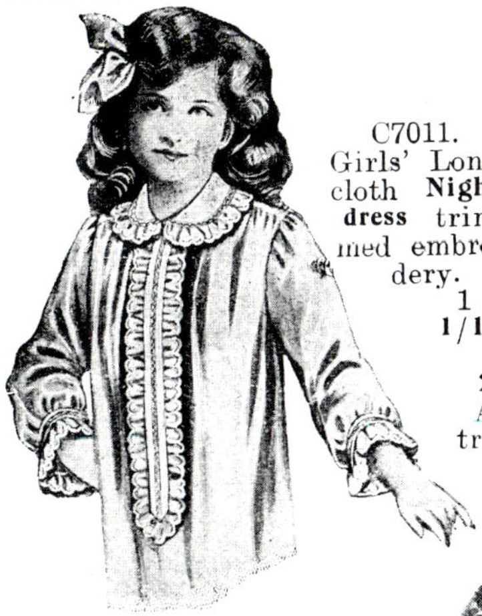

C7011.
Girls' Long-cloth **Nightdress** trimmed embroidery.

1	2	3	4	5	6	7	8	9
1/11¾	2/3¾	2/6¾	2/8¾	2/9½	2/11½	3/3¾	3/6¾	3/9¾

Also Nainsook Lace trimmed at same Pric.s.

C7012.—Trimmed Valenciennes Lace and Swiss Ribbon Insertion, French Knee-band.

00	0	1	2	3	4	5	6	7	8	9
1/3¾	1/4¾	1/6¾	1/8½	1/9¾	1/11¾	2/2½	2/4½	2/6¾	2/9¾	2/11¾

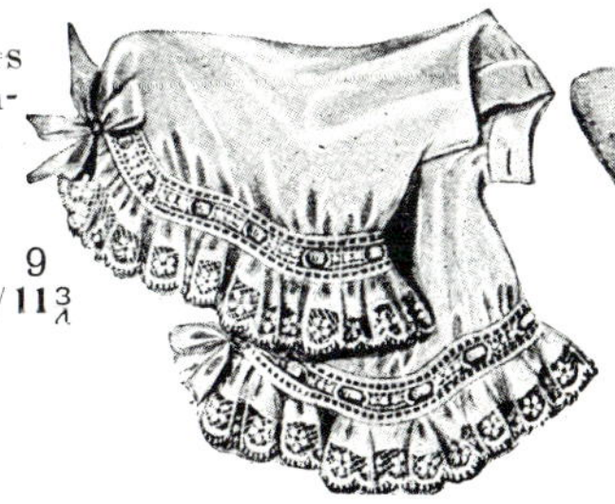

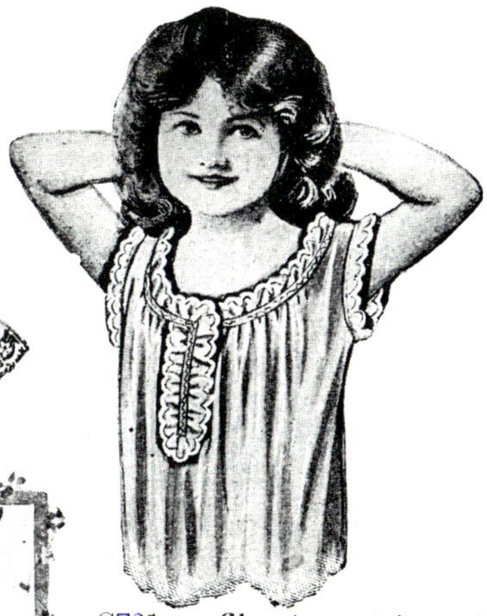

C7013.—**Chemise**, trimmed Button-hole Stitch.

1	2	3	4	5	6	7	8	9
1/2¾	1/4¾	1/6¾	1/8½	1/9¾	1/11¾	2/3¾	2/4¾	2/6¾

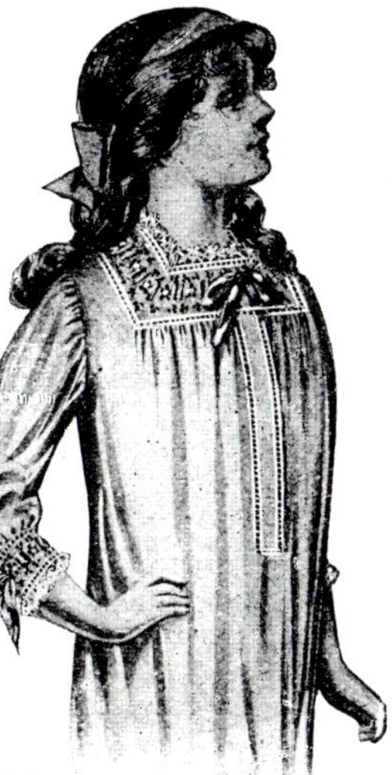

C7014.
Girl's Square Neck **Nightdress** trimmed fine wide Swiss Ribbon insertion, edged Real Torchon Lace.

Sizes 1	2	3	4	5	6	7	8	9
3/11¾	4/3¾	4/8¾	4/11½	5/6½	5/11½	6/6½	6/11½	7/6½

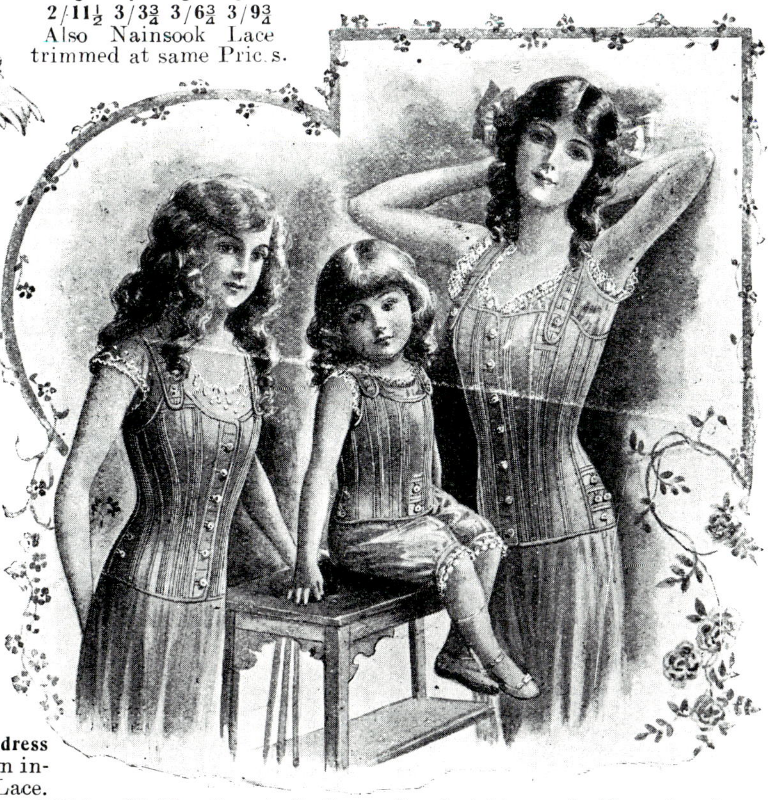

C7015.—**Pliable Corset Bodices**, Comfortable and Hygenic, in Dove.

Young Ladies, 19 in. to 28 in.	Price 2/11¾
Maids, 19 in. to 28 in.	Price 2/6¾
Girls, 20 in. to 26 in.	Price 1/11¾
Childs, 20 in. to 26 in.	Price 1/9¾
Infants, 20 in. to 26 in.	Price 1/6¾

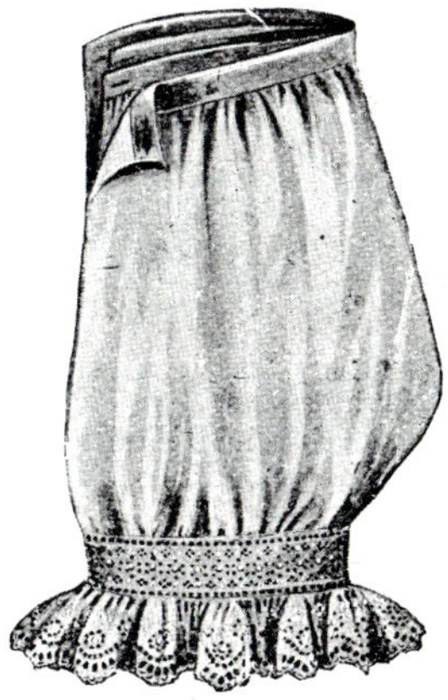

C7016.—**Knickers** trimmed fine Embroidery and Insertion Kneeband.

00	0	1	2	3	4
1/9¾	1/11¾	2/2½	2/3¾	2/4¾	2/6¾

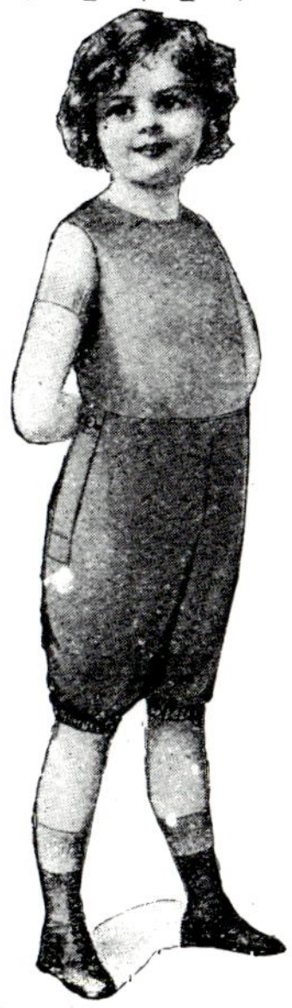

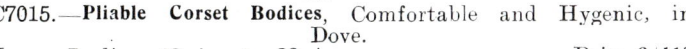

C7017. — Princess **Knickers**, new style. In Navy stockingette, with Sateen Bodice.

Sizes 0	1	2	3	4	5
1/11¾	2/1¾	2/3¾	2/4¾	2/6¾	2/9¾

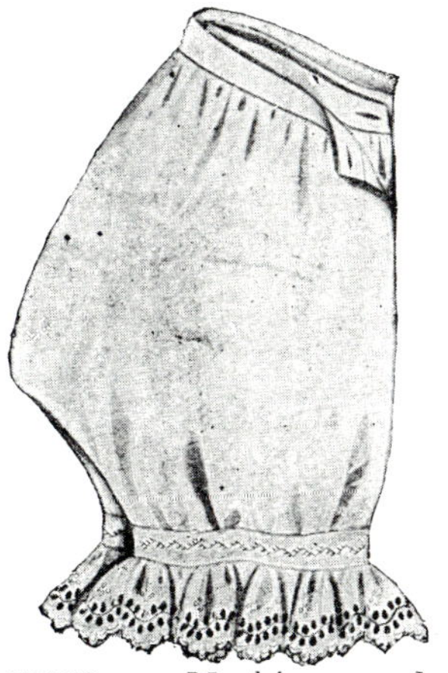

C7018. — Machine made, trimmed fine embroidery, Feathered Knee Band.

00	0	1	2	3	4	5	6	7	8	9
10¾d.	1/0¾	1/2¾	1/4¾	1/6¾	1/8¾	1/9¾	1/11¾	2/3¾	2/4¾	2/6¾

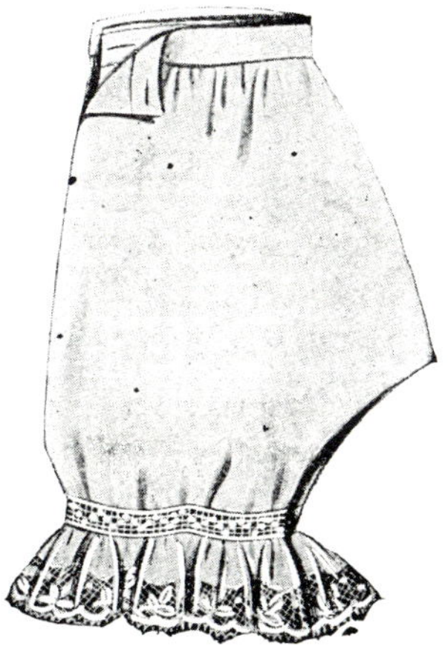

C7019. — Hand-made trimmed Valenciennes Lace.

0	1	2	3	4	5	6	7	8	9
1/6¾	1/11¾	1/11¾	2/3¾	2/6¾	2/9¾	2/11¾	3/3¾	3/6¾	3/9¾

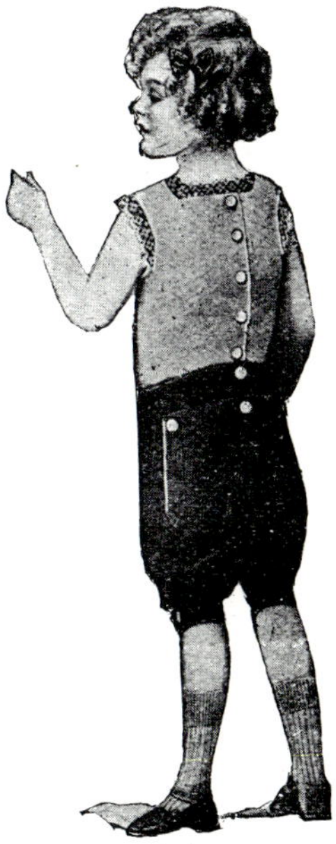

C7020.—Children's Golf **Knickers**. In Navy and Cream Stockingette.

Sizes 2	3	4	5	6	7	8
1/6¾	1/9¾	1/9¾	1/11¾	1/11¾	2/3¾	2/6¾

BABY LINEN DEPARTMENT.

BL7111.
LAYETTE No. 1.
3 GUINEAS.

		s.	d.
3 Swaithes	4$\frac{3}{4}$d.	1	2$\frac{1}{4}$
3 Wrapper Vests ...	1/0$\frac{3}{4}$	3	2$\frac{1}{4}$
3 Night Flannels ...	1/11$\frac{3}{4}$	5	11$\frac{1}{4}$
3 Day Flannels ...	1/11$\frac{3}{4}$	5	11$\frac{1}{4}$
4 Night Gowns ...	1/11$\frac{3}{4}$	7	11
2 Day Gowns ...	1/11$\frac{3}{4}$	3	11$\frac{1}{2}$
2 Day Gowns	2/11$\frac{3}{4}$	5	11$\frac{1}{2}$
1 doz. Turk-Napkins	3/6	3	6
1 doz. Turk-Napkins	4/6	4	6
Hood or Hat	2/11	2	11
1 Veil	1/0$\frac{3}{4}$	1	0$\frac{3}{4}$
1 Robe	6/11$\frac{1}{2}$	6	11$\frac{1}{2}$
1 Cloak	9/11$\frac{1}{2}$	9	11$\frac{1}{2}$
		£3 3	0

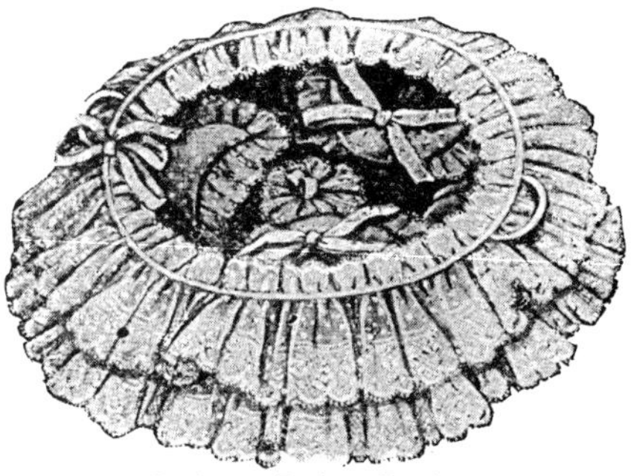

BL7112.—**Dainty Baby Baskets**, trimmed Spot Muslin, lined Sateen, edged Valenciennes Lace and Ribbon bows. **8/11, 10/11, 12/11**

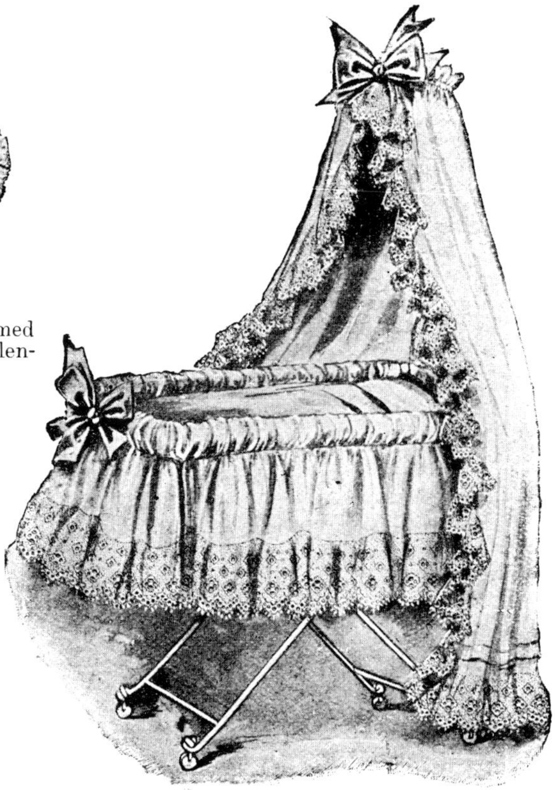

BL7113.—**Trimmed Cot**, all white or white over colours, plain or spot Muslin, trimmed lace with wide satin Ribbon. Price **3$\frac{1}{2}$ Guineas.**

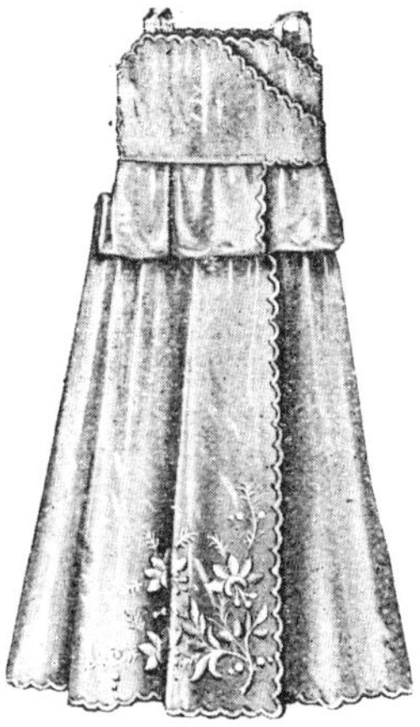

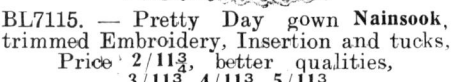

BL7114. — Infant's **Long Flannels**, Embroidered, **3/11$\frac{3}{4}$, 4/11$\frac{3}{4}$, 5/11$\frac{3}{4}$**. Also Plain Style **1/11$\frac{3}{4}$, 2/6$\frac{3}{4}$, 2/11$\frac{3}{4}$**

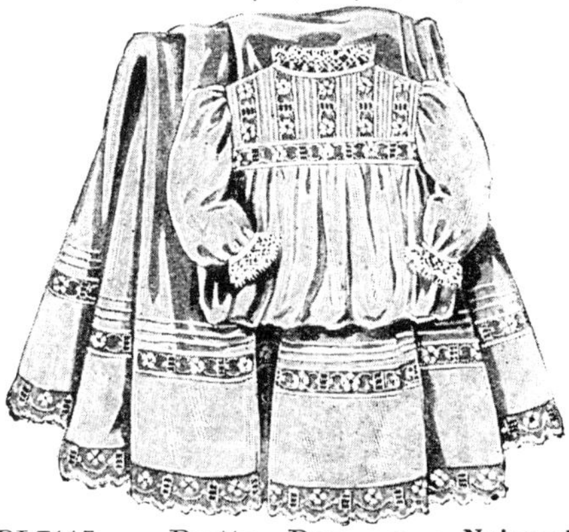

BL7115. — Pretty Day gown **Nainsook**, trimmed Embroidery, Insertion and tucks, Price **2/11$\frac{3}{4}$**, better qualities, **3/11$\frac{3}{4}$, 4/11$\frac{3}{4}$, 5/11$\frac{3}{4}$**

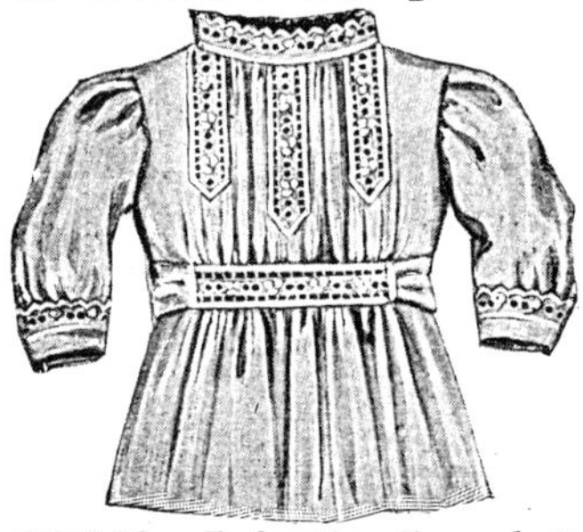

BL7116.—Infant's Longcloth **Night Gown**, good long cloth, trimmed Embroidery, Hand Sewn. Price **2/11$\frac{3}{4}$**

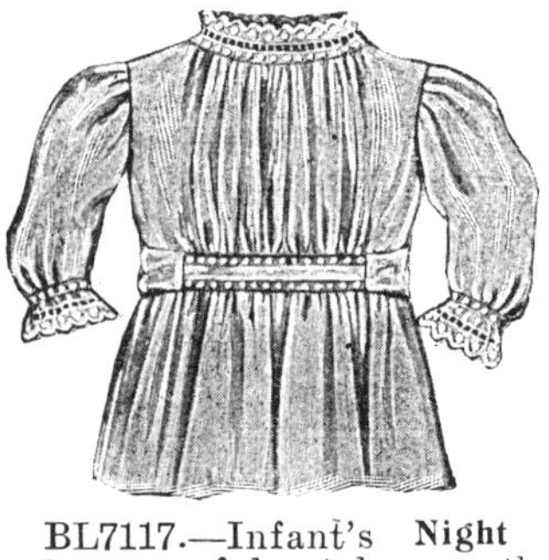

BL7117.—Infant's **Night Gown**, useful style, neatly trimmed. Price **1/6$\frac{3}{4}$**, better qualities **1/11$\frac{3}{4}$, 2/11$\frac{3}{4}$, 3/11$\frac{3}{4}$**

> ## COTS AND BASKETS.
>
> Any Design made to order in our own workroom.
>
> *Estimates and patterns post free.*

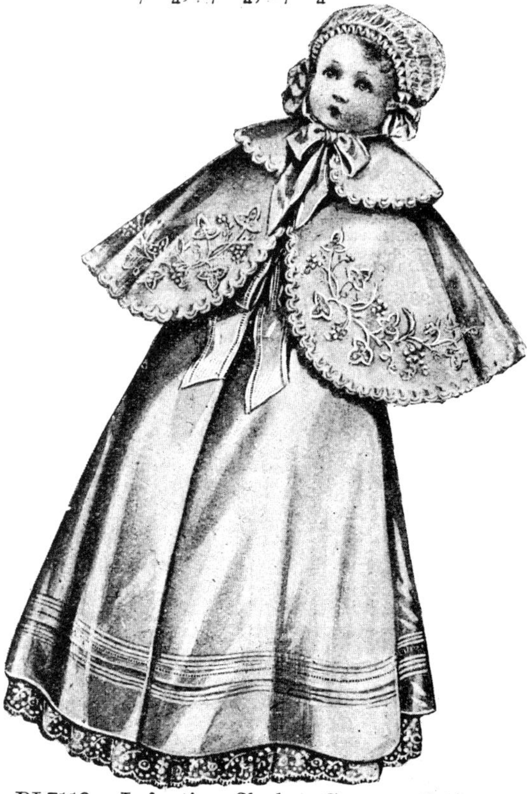

BL7118.—Infant's **Cloak**, Cream Cashmere, Dainty design. Price **14/11**, other qualities, various styles, **10/11, 12/11, 15/11, 18/11, 21/0**

BL7119. **LAYETTE No. 2.**
5 GUINEAS.

		£	s.	d.
3 Swaithes	6$\frac{3}{4}$d.		1	8$\frac{3}{4}$
3 Wrapper Vests ...	1/0$\frac{3}{4}$		3	2$\frac{1}{4}$
3 Night Flannels ...	1/11$\frac{3}{4}$		5	11$\frac{1}{4}$
2 Day Flannels ...	2/6$\frac{3}{4}$		5	1$\frac{1}{2}$
1 Day Flannel Embd.	2/11$\frac{3}{4}$		2	11$\frac{3}{4}$
2 Night Gowns ...	1/11$\frac{3}{4}$		3	11$\frac{1}{2}$
2 Night Gowns ...	2/11$\frac{3}{4}$		5	11$\frac{1}{2}$
2 Day Gowns	2/6$\frac{3}{4}$		5	1$\frac{1}{2}$
2 Day Gowns	2/11$\frac{3}{4}$		5	11$\frac{1}{2}$
2 doz. Napkins	3/11$\frac{3}{4}$		7	11$\frac{1}{2}$
1 doz. Napkins	4/11$\frac{1}{2}$		4	11$\frac{1}{2}$
1 Head Flannel ...	1/11$\frac{1}{2}$		1	11$\frac{1}{2}$
1 Long Slip	1/11$\frac{3}{4}$		1	11$\frac{3}{4}$
1 Long Slip	2/11$\frac{3}{4}$		2	11$\frac{3}{4}$
1 Christening Robe ...	16/11		16	11
1 Cloak	21/9	1	1	9
Hood or Hat	3/11$\frac{1}{2}$		3	11$\frac{1}{2}$
1 Veil	1/6$\frac{3}{4}$		1	6$\frac{3}{4}$
1 Bib	1/0$\frac{3}{4}$		1	0$\frac{3}{4}$
		£5	5	0

OUR TOY PAGES, 235-240, WILL PROBABLY INTEREST YOU.

Above: A fascinating group showing children of various ages including two babies in long mantles with capes. Perhaps a Christening party?

Above right: Two sisters in 1907. The eldest has put up her hair which she was proudly able to sit on.

Right: A 10-weeks-old baby in long clothes, woollen jacket and bib, 1908.

Below: A baby in long clothes with his mother in 1908.

Above: The hair is finally 'up' with the addition of two attractive black bows. A very pretty blouse is enhanced by an 'art nouveau' pendant of enamelled blue bird's wings with a mother-of-pearl drop, c1908.

Some of the various boy's suits of the period 1900-1914: (a) The Clyde Suit 3-6 years made of twill serge or homespun tweed — price about 8/6d (b) A ready-made Rugby suit of serge or tweed, up to 14 years, 22/-; (c) The Cambridge suit, up to 17 years, in blue or black serges or Scotch or West of England tweed, 27/6d to 34/6d; (d) A Reefing jacket worn from 3-10 years, of navy blue nap with gilt anchor buttons. (e) An Eton suit, 25/- to 34/- worn from 9-17 years: Grey hair-line trousers, the coat of black serge by day or black vicuna in the evenings. Black twill waistcoats by day, white Marcella in the evenings;
P. Stevenson

(f) The Jack Tar suit in navy blue rough serge, 25/9d; or white drill, 9/9d to 12/9d, 3-11 years;
(g) Cricketing or tennis outfit;
(h) Parisian suit in fancy tweed or black or blue velveteen c21/- about 7-9 years. *P. Stevenson*

Above left: Freda Evans on her Christening day aged four.

Above: Boys, girls and dolls in 1908.

Left: Joyce Rowley wearing a sailor blouse and pleated skirt, her sister Betty in white-embroidered muslin, and her mother, Eveline, in a smart dark braided dress.

Below: Upper class Peruvian children of Spanish descent — Rosita Maria and Salvador — 1911. *Philippa J. Archer*

FRANK BENTALL — Surrey's Premier Store. — Kingston on Thames.

Raphael Tuck & Sons' Publications.

A delightful Novelty for Children.

TY21311.—PICTURE BUILDING SERIES.

3 in. box, Price 1/4½
2 in. box, Price 10½d.

TRADE MARK.

Containing beautiful Coloured Pictures to be taken to pieces and put together again.

TY21312.—**Father Tuck's Nursery Rockers**, the delight of the nursery, Price, 10½d. per box.

TY21313.—The Royal Series of Dressing Dolls. Each Doll complete with four dresses and four hats in box.
Price 10½d.

TY21314.— **Father Tuck's Animals and Riders**, 100 distinct changes. Price, 10½d. per box.

TY21317.—**Gigantic Reliefs** in boxes. Prices dren. Price 10½d. per Box.

TY21316.—Series I.—Wild Animals. Series II.—Domestic Animals. Series III.—Beautiful Birds. Price 9d. per box.

TY21317.—**Gigantic Reliefs** in boxes. Prices from 10½d. to 3/6.

TUCK'S POST CARDS—most welcome and up-to-date.

PAPER PATTERNS AT HALF PRICE.

The Coupon on opposite page entitles you to one Paper Pattern of any of these designs in any size at Half-Price.—Ladies' Patterns, 3d. Children's, 2d.

15,603　　15,602　　15,971　　15,941 (4-gore) Matron's

Paper Patterns of these designs are obtainable in sizes of 22, 24, 26, and 28 inch. waist. Nos 15,602, 15,941, & 14,644 are also obtainable in sizes of 30 and 34 inch waist. Price 6d. each—with Coupon, price 3d.

No matter what you want in the way of a Paper Pattern, you are sure to be able to get it at our Paper Pattern Department.

In our Paper Pattern Department we have always in stock Patterns of over 2000 different designs for babies and children, in sizes to suit all figures and ages.

15,989　　15,783 (6-gore)　　15,974　　15,639 (4-Gore)　　14,644

FRANK BENTALL — 60 Separate Departments. — KINGSTON ON THAMES.

BOOK DEPARTMENT

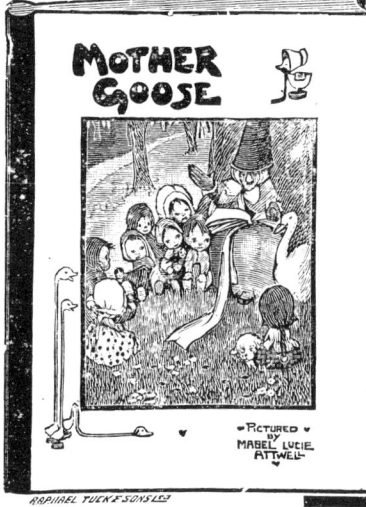

Printing, Die Sinking, Relief Stamping, Engraving, Etc., at very low Prices.

Write for Sample Book of Note Paper. Sent free on receipt of Post Card.

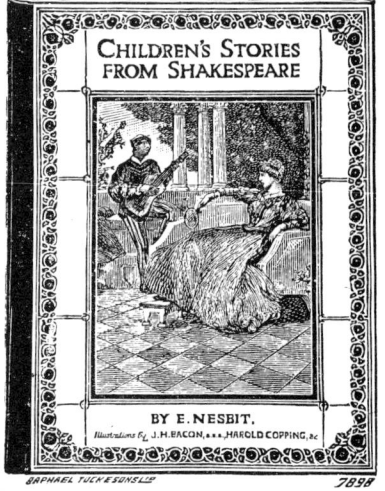

BK21411.—"Friends of Ours," entertaining animal stories with numerous Illustrations, Price 6d. net.

BK21412.—"Mother Goose," popular nursery rhymes, Illustrated in colours and Black and White, 144 pages, Price, 3/6 net.

BK21413.—Children's Stories from Shakespeare, Illustrated by J. H. Bacon, A.R.A., Harold Copping, etc., Price 3/6

BK21414.—"Farm Friends," Painting Book complete with Paints, Price, 6d. net.

BK21415.—Animal Postcard Painting Book, complete with paints, price 1/- net.

BK21416.—"Old Friends' Stories," with Illustrations in colours. Price 6d. net.

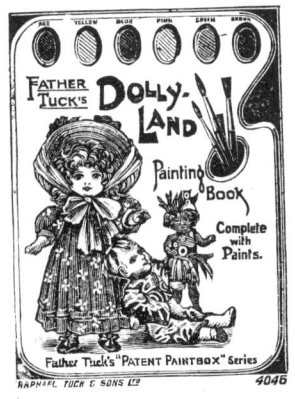

BK21417.—"Dolly-Land," Painting Book, complete with paints, Price 6d. net.

BK21418.—"Animal Pictures," postcard painting book, Price, 1/0 net.

BK21419.—"Kindergarten" painting book, complete with paints, Price, 6d. net.

Rewards' Books for School, Prizes a Speciality.

Toy Books and Annuals at lowest Discount Prices.

BK21420.—"Bird Life," painting book, Price, 6d. net.

BK21421.—Painting Album, studies of landscapes by A. Barraud, Price, 1/0 net.

BK21422.—"The Happy Family," delightful stories in prose and verse, by well known writers, Illustrated by Louis Wain, Price, 3/6 net.

WE GIVE OUR PLEDGE FOR SATISFACTION IN EVERY ORDER.

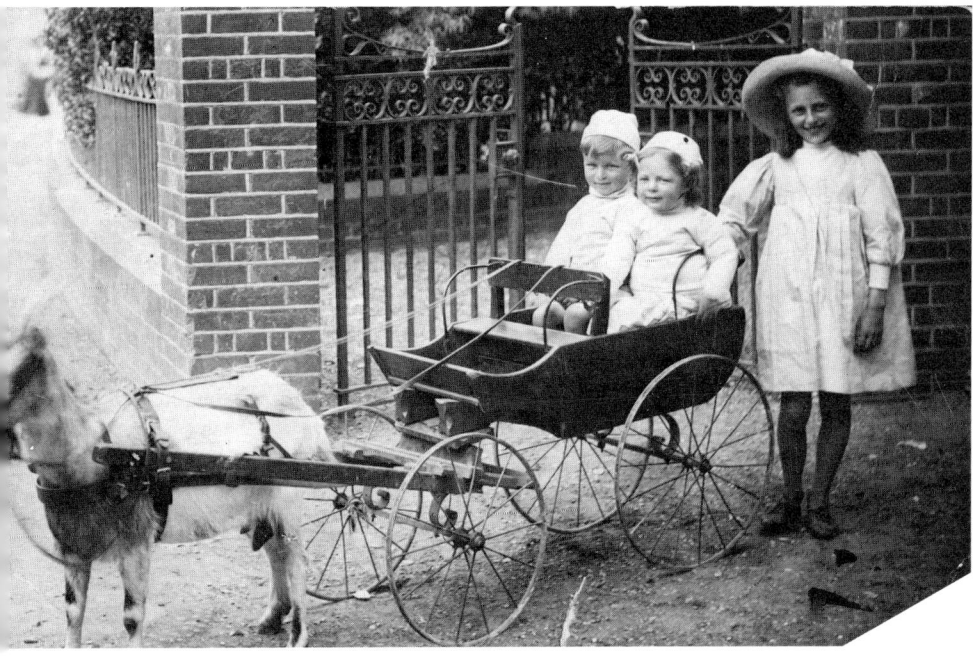

Above: Ethel, Cyril and Helen Clarke at Hunstanton in 1910 with a fascinating goat cart.

Right: These sentimental child studies for postcards were very popular at this time.

Below right: A comic postcard of 1912, but interesting as it shows the way in which children's dresses and overalls were so frequently made with tucks to allow for growth.

Below: Another example of the sentimentalised child on a postcard, in this case a little girl in tulle and lilies of the valley.

FRANK BENTALL — PERFECT SATISFACTION OR MONEY RETURNED. — Kingston on Thames.

TOY DEPARTMENT.

TY95.—**Specially Made Carriage-Finish Pram.** Reversible Hood in Best Steel Strap Hung. Cee Springs. Measures 23½in. by 12in. on top. **26/9**

TY96.—**The New Opened Room Dolls' House.**

28in. high,	27in. wide,	15in. deep,	10/6
32 ,,	29½ ,,	15½ ,,	16/9
34 ,,	32 ,,	17 ,,	20/9

TY97.—**The New Model.** Measurement of Body, 20in. by 10in. on top. Steel Hub, 12 by 8. Rubber Tyred Wheels, with China Handle, **12/6**

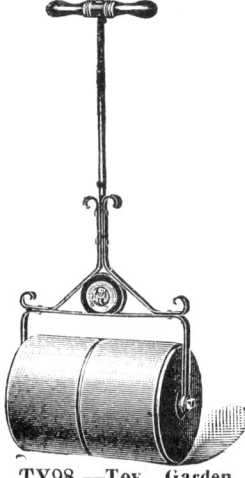

TY98.—**Toy Garden Roller.** Nicely Painted and Lined. Height to Handle, 26in. 3/6½; 29in., 4/9½; 35in. 6/6½

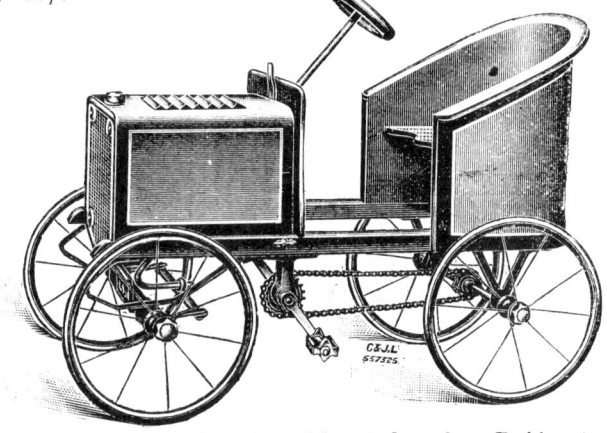

TY99.—**Specially Made Motor.** Mounted on four Rubber-tyred wheels, 12in. diameter, and is finished in Navy or Green. Highly Coach Finish. As Illustration, **24/6**. Ditto fitted with one horn and one lamp. **26/9**

TY100.—**Specially Made Push Car.** Mounted on Light Iron Spider Wheels. Height to Handle, 30in. **5/11½**

TY101.—**The New Motor Car.** Artillery Wheels, with wired-on rubber tyres. Long step board and wings and adjustable seat. Fitted with lamp and horn, **41/6**

TY102.—**The Clarence Toy Pram.** Extra large Model. Measurement, 28in. by 13in. on top, 14in. by 10in. rubber wheels. Nicely finished throughout. Supplied in Navy or Dark Green. **22/6**

A large collection of Dolls, Games, Building and Picture Bricks, Balls, Boats, Trains, Soldiers, Fur Animals and Clock-work Toys always in stock at very low prices.

ENGLISH MADE TOYS A SPECIALITY.

NEW BABY CARS.

F27211.—**Polished Birch,** Spindle Back, Canvas Seat, **9/11**

F27212.—**Polished Walnut Colour.** Back and Seat Upholstered Rexine Leather Cloth, **17/11**

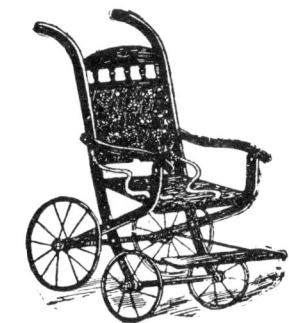

F27213.—**Polished Birch.** Carpet Back, Seat and Extension, **11/9**

F27214.—**Polished Birch.** Carpet Back and Seat, **11/9**

F27215.—**Polished Birch.** Fancy Cane Back and Seat **14/11**

F27216.—**Polished Birch.** Fancy Cane Back and Seat. Adjustable Back, which works with foot rest. **19/11**

F27217.—**Polished Birch.** Back and Carpet Seat, **10/11**

F27218.—**Polished Birch.** Reversible Back and Seat. Two-position Car, **13/6**

F27219.—**Polished Walnut Colour.** Back Upholstered Rexine Leather Cloth. **16/11**

F27220.—**Polished Walnut Colour.** Upholstered Rexine Leather Cloth, **16/11**

F27221.—**Polished Birch.** Carpet Back and Seat. Folds into small compass.

Folded.

F27222.—**Polished Birch.** Carpet Back and Seat. With Holland Canopy. Complete **12/11**

F27223.—**Polished Walnut Colour.** Upholstered Moquette Velvet, **16/11**

F27224.—**Polished Birch.** Carpet Seat and Extension. Four-position Car, **13/6**

F27225.—**Polished Birch.** Carpet Seat and Arms. Velvet Side Wings, **11/9**

READ GUARANTEE ON INSIDE BACK COVER.

FRANK BENTALL
LUNCHEON AND TEA ROOM FIRST FLOOR.
KINGSTON ON THAMES.

ADJUSTABLE BABY CHAIRS.
NEW DESIGNS OF ADJUSTABLE BABY CHAIRS.

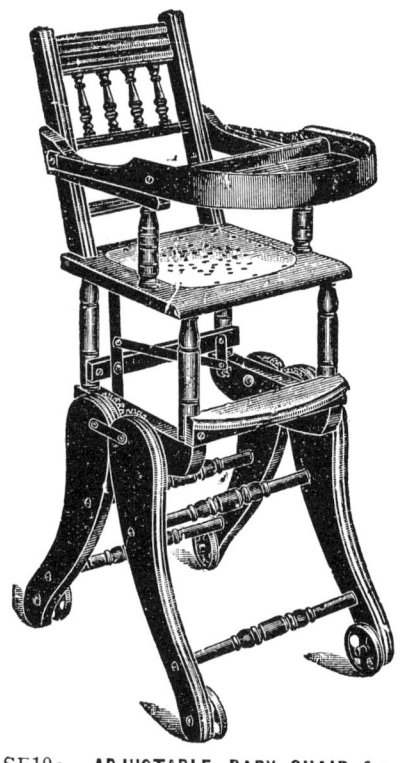

SF19A.—**ADJUSTABLE BABY CHAIR**, four positions, stained Walnut or Mahogany colour, with playboard, 17/11

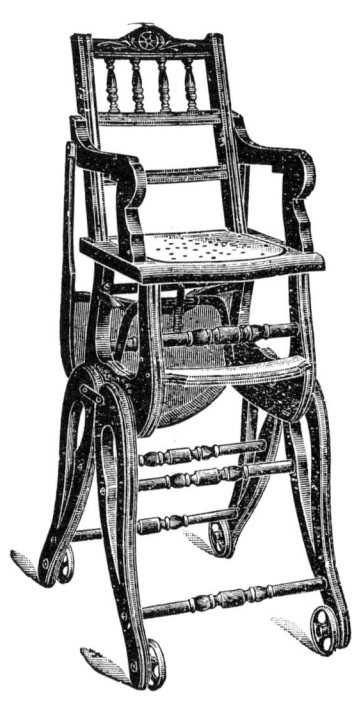

SF19.—**ADJUSTABLE BABY CHAIR**, as illustration, four positions, stained Walnut colour, Baluster Back, 13/11

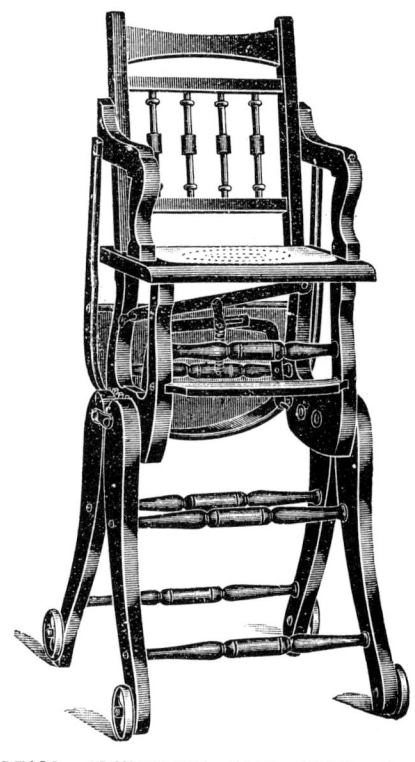

SF126.—**ADJUSTABLE BABY CHAIR**, four positions, side lever, Walnut or Mahogany colour, as illustration, 12/6
With embossed velvet back, 14/11

SF84.—**ADJUSTABLE BABY CHAIR**, four positions (see positions) stained Walnut colour. 17/11

- - Have you visited our - -
LUNCHEON AND TEA ROOM
yet? You will be charmed with it.

Make a Point of Writing to-day for Samples of Our Dress Materials in Cotton, Woollen, or Silks.

We offer you the Best Value obtainable.

Our Stock is continually changing.

New Novelties Arrive Daily. We guarantee to please you or will return your Cash in full.

SF84A.—**CARRIAGE POSITION.** 17/11

REMOVALS TO ALL PARTS OF THE GLOBE.

Right: Baby of 8 months in short clothes, 1911.

Below: Proud father and mother with their first child taking its first steps.

Left and above: A toddler in muslin dress, jacket and bonnet.

Above right: Small girl of 18 months between 1912 and 1913 standing on a sundial.

Right: Paddling and building sandcastles at Newquay in 1913. Note the paddling drawers of fine oilskin or rubber and little girls with dresses tucked into knickers.

Above far left: Running down the passage!

Above left: Warmly clad for winter in white furry coat, hat, muff and gaiters in 1913. In this outfit she was known as 'The little polar bear'.

Above: This little girl's hair simply would not grow c1913.

Left: A family party with a goat cart at Hunstanton in 1914. Note Grandmama's bonnet and mother's flowered hat.

Left: At Newquay on a donkey.

Below left: Asleep in the pushcart 1913.

Below: Paddling with practical bloomers c1914.

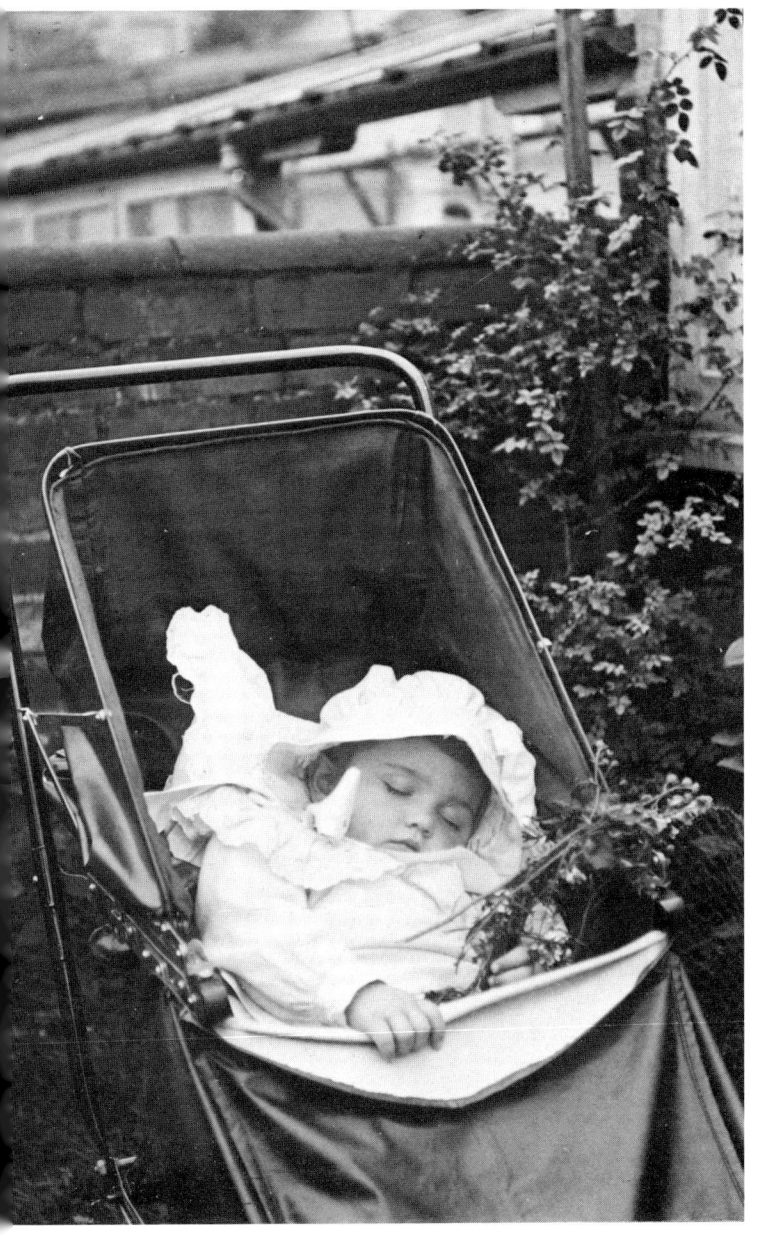

Men

Above: In 1899 motoring could be attended by great hazards and the cars were generally open.
Mary Evans Picture Library

Top: Arliss Haydon Carter taken on the occasion of his engagement, 1899.

Above: Philip de la Garde of Exeter in a light summer suit and light hat about 1900. A clever painter, and a purser in the Navy.

Left: The popular frock coat, worn in 1897 and on. This outfit could be worn by a bridegroom and best man who were dressed alike. It is a black frock coat with revers faced with black silk worn over a light double-breasted waistcoat. The gloves would be of pale tan kid and the trousers would be of grey striped cashmere. A black silk hat, black leather boots or shoes, spats, and a light tie and silver topped cane completed the outfit. *P. Stevenson*

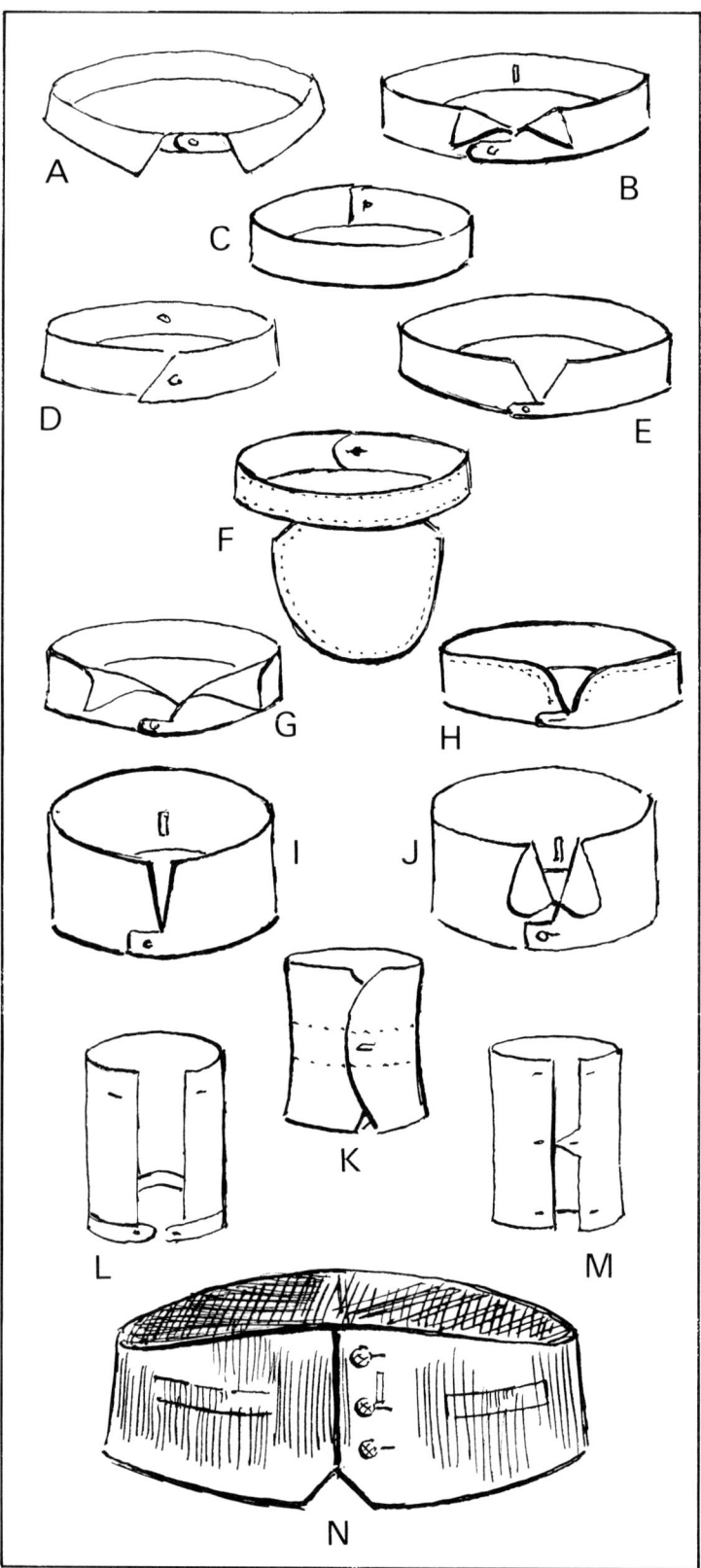

Above: A few of the extraordinary number of collars, all with special names, are shown together with a few cuffs: (a) the Shakespeare; (b) the Edinburgh; (c) Durham; (d) Windsor; (e) Connaught; (f) Clerical; (g) Prince; (h) Ascot; (i) Royal S; (j) Royal Oak; (k) The Lord Lytton cuff; (l) The American cuff; (m) The Westminster cuff; (n) A short waistcoat for use in the tropics in the evening of silk or surah, (note slit for watchchain). *P. Stevenson*

Right: The Morning Coat of 1897, in black and often worn with a light waistcoat, but a black waistcoat worn for mourning. Slight differences in length, and number of buttons should be noted as time goes on. *P. Stevenson*

FRANK BENTALL — Write, Call or Phone. — KINGSTON ON THAMES.

WALKING STICKS.

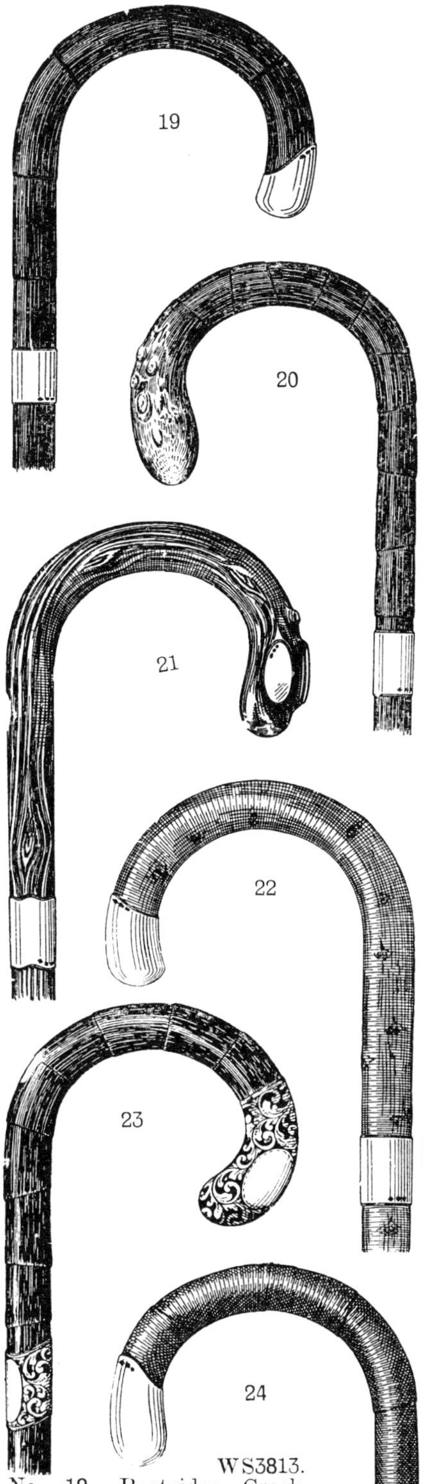

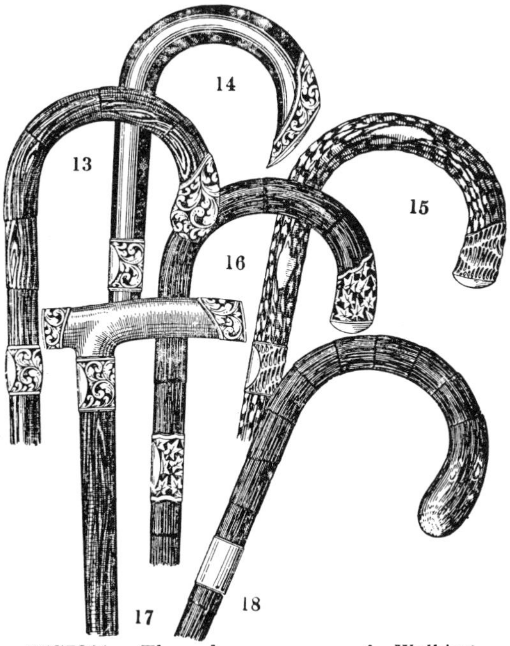

WS3811.—The above group of Walking Sticks, 7/6 each.
No. 13.—Crocus Wood. Silver Nose and Band.
No. 14.—Ebony Crook. Chased silver Nose and Band.
No. 15.—Lucian. Fine silver Nose, Band and Cap.
No. 16.—Partridge Crook. Chased silver Nose and Band.
No. 17.—Figured Ebony Horn Crutch. Silver Nose and Band.
No. 18.—Plain Partridge Crook. Silver Band.

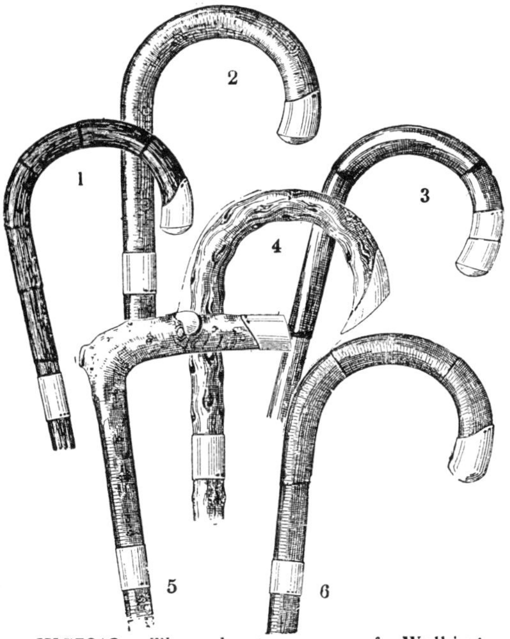

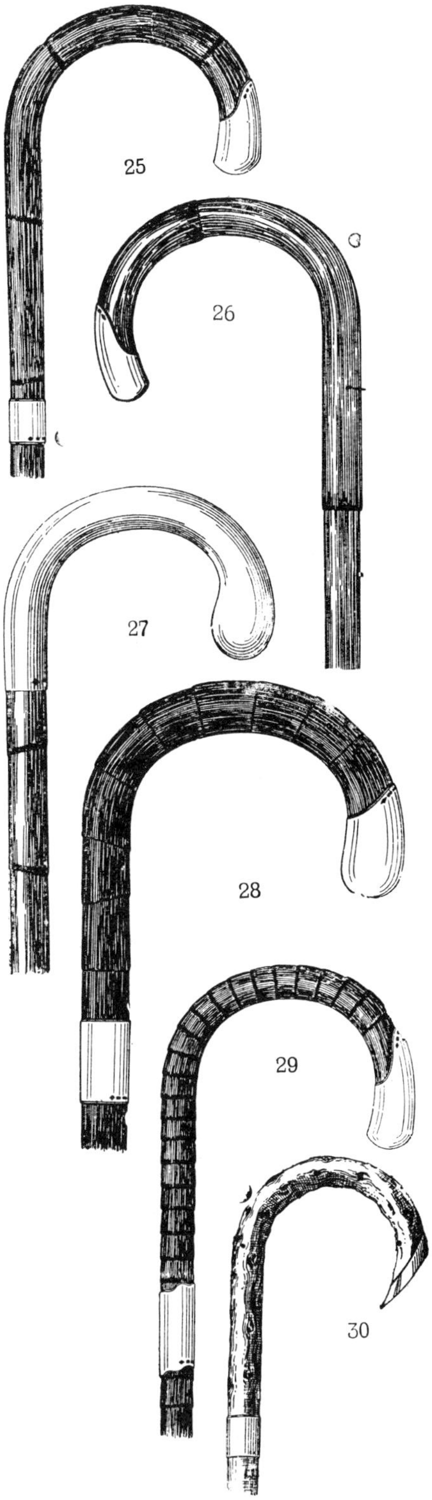

WS3813.
No. 19.—Partridge Crook Silver Nose and Band 4/-
No. 20.—Partridge Crook, Silver Band 6/-
No. 21.—Crocus Crook, Silver Plates and Band 5/-
No. 22.—Cherry, Silver Nose and Band 3/-
No. 23.—Partridge, Silver Nose and Band 12/6
No. 24.—Panama, Silver Nose 3/-

WS3812.—The above group of Walking Sticks, 2/9 each.
No. 1.—Partridge. Silver Nose and Band.
No. 2.—Cherry, Silver Nose and Band.
No. 3.—Bahama. Silver Nose.
No. 4.—Congo. Silver Nose and Band.
No. 5.—Ashplant. Silver Nose and Band.
No. 6.—Panama. Silver Nose and Band.

WS3814
No. 25.—Partridge Crook, Silver Nose and Band 3/-
No. 26.—Bahama Crook, Silver Nose 3/-
No. 27.—Partridge Silver Crook 10/6
No. 28.—Partridge Silver Nose and Band 12/6
No. 29.—Partridge Silver Nose and Band 4/-
No. 30.—Congo Silver Nose and Band 3/-

Right: A smoking jacket and a dressing jacket for wearing indoors, 1899. *P. Stevenson*

Below: Richard Jerman, about 1900, showing the typical beard and haircut made popular by Edward VII.

Below right: The younger Anglican clergymen were generally clean shaven, possibly due to the influence of the Oxford movement.

Left: Sally and Walter Hookway on the occasion of their Golden wedding in 1901. He resembles Edward VII but she wears a Victorian bonnet and mantle trimmed with jet bugles. The feather boa is an Edwardian touch.

Left: The single or double-breasted Ulster. *P. Stevenson*

Right: The Paddock or Paletot. *P. Stevenson*

Above: The Lounge morning coat from 1895 onwards.
P. Stevenson

Right: The black Evening dress suit with white piqué (stiffened) shirt. The trousers sometimes had braid down the side of the legs. Gloves were worn of cream or white stitched in black. White ties were generally worn. *P. Stevenson*

Right: Walter Jerman, a smart young man in 1905. Note the collar, cravat, tie and tiepin and light waistcoat.

Above: The golf suit of 1896 onwards but changes will be noticed in later versions.
Philippa J. Archer

Right: An informal outfit for country wear.
Philippa J. Archer

Above: Frederick Richard Rowley, Curator of the Royal Albert Memorial Museum, Exeter, dressed for walking on Dartmoor in a Norfolk suit, but with a waxed moustache and pince-nez, 1905.

Far left: Amyas Jerman, aged 20, wearing a waistcoat with a revers and very stiff collar.

Left: His twin brother in a similar suit and collar in 1906. Here the jacket is buttoned.

Above: George Woolway ARCA, first principal of St Martin's School of Art, London, as a young man.

A

Above: Possibly a group of city clerks about 1906. One actually wears a cap and soft collar and brown shoes!

Left: (a) The Covert coat; the Chesterfield was like the Covert but came to the knees; (b) Another version of the Lounge suit, showing lounge jacket; (c) The furlined overcoat which sometimes had fur cuffs as well as a fur collar, and according to the fur used was priced from £8.10s, eg: Hamster or genette, to Canadian Sable at £170. A hamster-lined coat with a collar of a fur called electric seal would be priced at £8.10s and a musquash-lined coat with a collar of natural beaver would cost £13.10s or £1 more for an astrachan collar. *P. Stevenson*

(a) American walking frock coat of 1900. Greater ease and comfort were expected in the cut than in England and more cloth was used and the trousers were cut looser and darted at the waist. Turn up trousers were popular which were said to derive from an Englishman turning up his trousers on a muddy day at Ascot; (b) Informal wear in 1907; (c) Shows an outfit for Palm Beach. It is obvious that Americans favoured less formal and more colourful clothes and accessories. *P. Stevenson*

Men's Apparel
For the Horse Show

❡ The attention of critical men is invited to the absolute correctness of our every requirement for formal wear, from the conventional full dress suit or overcoat to the least important accessory.

❡ The opportunities for the exercise of individual taste are among the surpassing features of the refined characteristic styles that find extensive representation in our displays of Men's Furnishings.

❡ Intelligent individual attention is given the selections for each line—always with a thorough knowledge of what is correct, always with especial reference to a perfectly harmonious relationship.

. . . .

❡ When time is a consideration, the constant readiness of our Men's Sections will prove of invaluable assistance.

Marshall Field *and* Company

Above: An example of American advertising for Marshall Field & Co in 1906.
The Mansell Collection

Top right: Walter Hookway on his 82nd birthday in 1907, but still a dandy and reminiscent of Edward VII.

Above right: This portrait photo shows an easier style of collar, but the cut of the beard and hair shows the King's influence; c1909.

Left: A very high stiff collar and highly buttoned dark suit c1908.

Right: A school leaver and ready for his first job!

Above left: Waxed moustaches (probably a German fashion) and a knitted tie c1909.

Above: Dr Hodgeson, the biologist on Scott's last expedition and curator of the Plymouth Museum c1912. He wears a cameo tie pin.

Left: Astley Clarke 1912. It was fashionable to be clean-shaven.

Right: Some of the 62 different types of hats and caps, all with special names, one or two are still being worn: 1 The soft felt or Homburg in black, dark or light brown, or drab made fashionable by the King; 2 The Deerstalker beloved of Sherlock Holmes; 3 The Straw Boater very popular until it was adopted by women, children and the 'lower classes'; 4 The Portland; 5 The Panama; 6 The Colonial; 7 The black Clerical; 8 The Clifford; 9 The Trent; 10 The Sutton; 11 The Balaclava sleeping cap; 12 The hand knit Tam o'Shanter worn informally by both sexes and all ages; 13 The Fishing hat; 14 The Deerstalker with a dish brim; 15 The Rutland; 16 The Sans Souci; 17 Tyrol; 18 A hard felt Topper; 19 Silk Top Hat; 20 The Hunting topper as worn by Lord Ribblesdale in his portrait by Sargent in the Tate Gallery; 21 Double Terai; 22 Cawnpore, as worn in India, ladies wore the same with light drapery round the crown; 23 The Graham, generally in light brown. A similar hat was the Derby popular in the US and with a higher crown. *P. Stevenson*

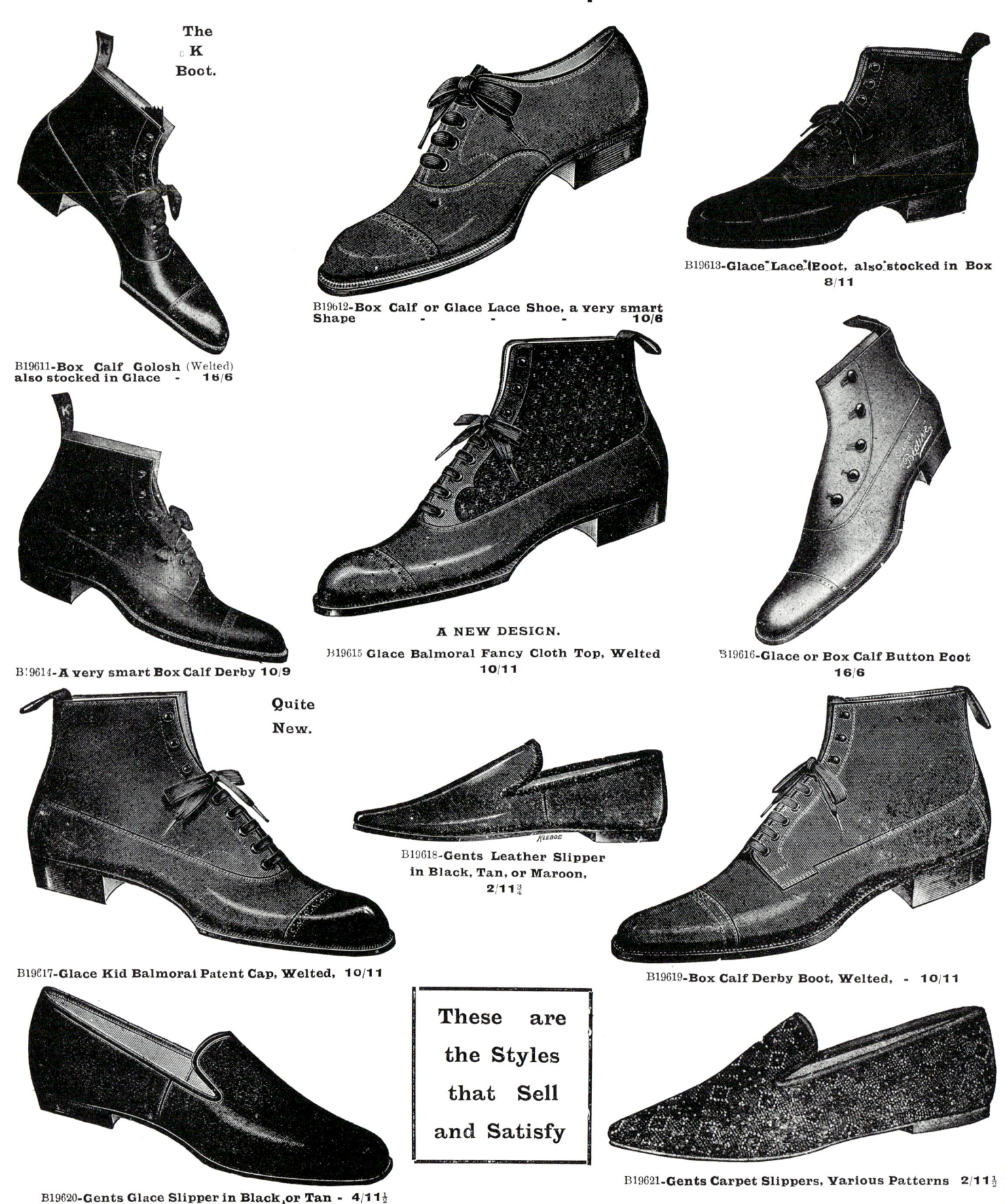

FRANK BENTALL

Write, Call or Phone. — KINGSTON ON THAMES.

BOOT AND SHOE DEPARTMENT—continued.

B19711-Chrome Football Boot with Instep Protecter - - - 10/6

B19712-Tan Newmarket Gaiter with Spring - 8/11

B19713-Gents' White Buck Cricket Boots 10/6 Better quality 12/6

B19714-Gents' Cycling Shoes in Tan or Black - - - 4/11½

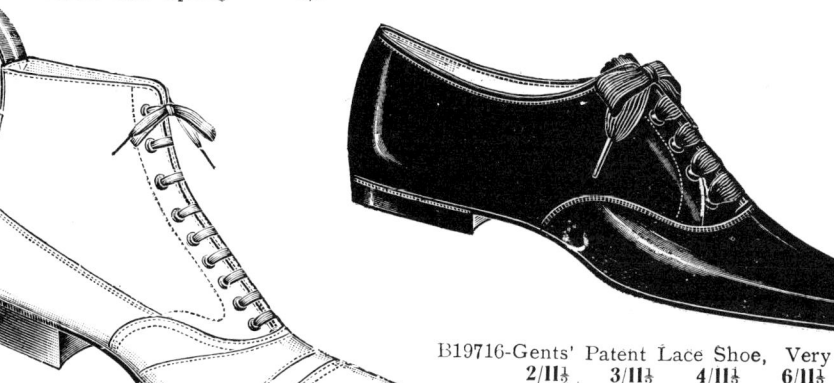

B19715-White Buck Cricket Boot - 8/11
A very Special Line.

B19716-Gents' Patent Lace Shoe, Very Smart
2/11½   3/11½   4/11½   6/11½

9717-Patent Dress Shoes   2/11½   3/11½   4/11½   6/11½

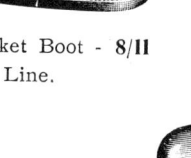

B19718-Gents Tennis Shoes in Brown or White
2/11½   3/11½   4/11½

B19719-Chrome Football Boot
5/11½   6/11½   7/11½

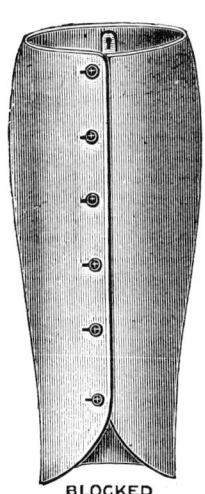

BLOCKED
B19720-Tan or Black Newmarket Gaiter 7/11

B19721-Tan Football Boots   4/11½   5/11½   6/11½
Boys'   3/11½   4/11½   5/11½

F2

Above far left: The actor Beerbohm Tree. A bright bow tie and loose coat over a dark suit.

Above left: Joseph Chamberlain in 1905.

Far left: Sir Henry Irving, the famous actor; he was knighted in 1895 and died in 1905.

Left: Gen Sir Redvers Buller and his medals! Famous for his relief of Ladysmith in the S African War. He died in 1908.

Above: From a photo of the German Emperor entitled 'The Royal Invalid HIM The German Emperor, King of Prussia, whose tour on the Mediterranean will include a visit to Gibraltar, 1904' He is shown wearing the uniform of the Death's Head Hussars. *P. Stevenson*

Above right: General Sir John French, Chief of the Imperial General Staff (1911-1914), created 1st Earl of Ypres in 1921.

Right: General Gripenberg, commander of the second Manchurian Army in October 1904. The Russo-Japanese War was in progress and several Russian generals had these unbelievable moustaches. *P. Stevenson*

Left: The King of the Bulgarians and his decorations!
Mary Evans Picture Library

Above far left: The uniform of the volunteers in S Africa c1907.

Above left: Khaki uniform and puttees in 1914.

Above: A radio officer in the Merchant Navy about 1913.

Left: Uniforms of World War 1.

Above right: An OTC camp at Birmingham — the Tent Crew.

Above far right: Military enthusiasm in 1914!

Right: Voluntary Aid Detachment uniform c1914–15.

Far right: A card from the French battlefield.

Courage brave défenseur je veillerai sur toi toujours

Left: Training for the signals in 1914.

Below: Signals Officers in training in England in 1914.